PROBLEMS OF REGIONAL ECONOMIC PLANNING

PROBLEMS OF REGIONAL
ECONOMIC PLANNING

* * *

J-R. BOUDEVILLE

**Professor of Economic Science
University of Paris**

EDINBURGH
AT THE UNIVERSITY PRESS

© EDINBURGH UNIVERSITY PRESS 1966
22 George Square Edinburgh
North America
Aldine Publishing Company
529 South Wabash Avenue, Chicago

ISBN 0 85224 052 X
Library of Congress
Catalog Card Number 65-1543
First Published 1966
Reprinted 1968, 1974

Printed in Great Britain by
Lewis Reprints Ltd.
(member of The Brown, Knight & Truscott Group)
London & Tonbridge

PREFACE

This short book is a revised and enlarged version of a series of six lectures I had the honour to deliver in the University of Edinburgh, by kind invitation of Professor A. J. Youngson.

The objective behind these chapters is to evoke the interest of a wider public about the notion of French prospective regional planning, and of the French economic thought on this subject. Therefore, the book is not only addressed to economic specialists but to all responsible industrialists and civil servants.

The three concepts of space in Chapter 1, as defined by Professor François Perroux — homogeneous, polarized and programming space — will be our guide throughout. The different economic tools advanced by the world's regional scientists are described and illustrated in Chapters 2 and 3 with reference to the three basic notions of space. The chief technical developments are included in Chapters 4 and 5, which deal with regional operational models. Finally, Chapters 6 and 7 briefly describe the fourth French Plan, the emphasis being on the functioning of regional planning, and consider some new aspects of the current fifth Plan.

I wish to acknowledge the friendly and stimulating encouragement which I received from Professor Youngson throughout. I am grateful to Mr Y. Yannoulis, who prepared English versions of the earlier chapters, and whose criticisms were of great help. My thanks also go to the Secretary to the Press, without whose editorial care and enlightened questions this book would never have been completed. However, I remain fully responsible for the inexactitudes which may appear in the text.

J-R. Boudeville

THE CONTENTS

1. Concepts and Definitions *page* 1

CONCEPTS OF SPACE, 1; HOMOGENEITY, POLARIZATION, AND FINALITY, 2; SPACE AND REGION, 3; MACRO AND MICRO-ECONOMICS, 6; HOMOGENEITY, 7; HOMOGENEOUS REGIONS, 8; POLARIZATION, 9; HIERARCHY OF CITIES, 10; BOUNDARY MOVEMENT, 11; PROSPECTIVE AND PROGRAMMING, 14; PROGRAMMING SPACE AND REGION, 16; CHOICE OF INSTRUMENTS, 18; REGIONAL AND NATIONAL HIERARCHY, 19.

2. The tools for regional economic studies *page* 22

EMPIRICAL FOUNDATIONS, 22; OBSERVATIONAL METHODS, 23; HOMOGENEITY ANALYSIS, 24; CORRELATION ANALYSIS, 26; POLARIZATION ANALYSIS, 27; FORMAL DESCRIPTION, 28; TENTATIVE EXPLORATORY RESEARCH, 30; DETERMINING REGIONAL BOUNDARIES, 32; BOUNDARIES OF HOMOGENEOUS REGIONS, 33; PLURALITY OF HETEROGENEOUS CHARACTERISTICS, 33; PLOTTING A HOMOGENEOUS REGION, 35; MOVEMENT OF BOUNDARIES, 36; BOUNDARIES OF POLARIZED REGIONS, 38; GRAPH ANALYSIS, 38; GRAVITATION ANALYSIS AND BOUNDARY MOVEMENT, 41; DYNAMIC ASPECTS OF BOUNDARY MOVEMENT, 44.

3. Regional economic programmes *page* 46

PROGRAMMING REGIONS AND DEVELOPMENT REGIONS, 46; REGIONALIZING A NATIONAL PLAN, 47; POLICY FOR SPONTANEOUS DEVELOPMENT, 48; RATIONAL IN-

CITATION POLICY, 49; DECENTRALIZED REGIONAL
PLANNING, 51; AUTONOMOUS PROGRAMMES, 51; DIS-
COVERING THE VARIABLES UNDERLYING GROWTH, 52;
REGIONAL POWERS, 55; NATIONAL CO-ORDINATION OF
REGIONAL PLANNING, 56; WELFARE, 57; SPHERES OF
INFLUENCE, 58; REGIONAL PROLETARIANISM, 62; EUR-
OPEAN CO-OPERATION, 64; INTER-REGIONAL CO-
OPERATION, 64; MEDIUM-TERM GROWTH, 65; FEDERAL
STATES AND REGIONAL SOLUTIONS, 67; LONG-TERM
REGIONAL GROWTH, 69.

4. Regional operational models   page 75
   I : *Regionalization Models and National Planning*
   IMPORTANCE OF OBJECTIVES, 75; REGIONALIZING
   EMPLOYMENT MODELS, 77; REGIONAL EMPLOYMENT
   MULTIPLIERS, 82; REGIONALIZATION OF INVESTMENT
   IN NATIONAL PLANNING, 85; REGIONALIZATION OF NAT-
   IONAL ACCOUNTING, 88; AGGREGATION OF NATIONAL
   MATRIX, 90; CONCENTRATION RATIOS, 92; AN ALTER-
   NATIVE METHOD, 94; THE AGRICULTURAL COMPLEX, 96;
   REGIONAL TRADE AND SUBSIDIES, 100.

5. Regional operational models   page 102
   II : *Autonomous Regional Development*
   AUTONOMOUS REGIONAL DEVELOPMENT, 102; REGIONAL
   AND NATIONAL GROWTH, 102; HETEROGENEOUS GROWTH
   MODELS, 103; POLARIZED GROWTH MODELS, 107; ALTER-
   NATIVE MODEL, 110; PROPULSIVE STRUCTURE, 112;
   POLARIZATION EFFECT, 113; SATELLITE INDUSTRY AND
   FORWARD LINKAGE, 115; OLIGOPOLISTIC CONCENTRA-
   TION, 117; A POLARIZATION ACTIVITY MODEL, 118;
   INTER-REGIONAL CONNECTIONS, 119; PROPULSIVE IN-
   DUSTRIES AND MUTATIONS OF STRUCTURE, 121; ARBI-
   TRATION BETWEEN REGIONS, 123; DIFFERENCES OF VALUE
   JUDGMENT, 124; INCREASE IN TOTAL RESOURCES, 126;

SOCIAL OVERHEAD CAPITAL, 129; CHOICE OF REGIONAL
OBJECTIVES, 130; INTEGRATION AND MULTIPLICITY OF
GOALS, 130; THE CONDORCET PROBLEM, 131.

6. The fourth French plan *page* 136

THE PROGRAMMERS AND THE DECISION, 137; MODERN-
IZATION COMMISSIONS, 137; ADMINISTRATIVE PROCED-
URE, 140; HOW EFFECTIVE IS FRENCH PLANNING? 141;
GENERAL CONSIDERATIONS, 141; SPECIAL INCENTIVES,
142; INCREASE IN ANNUAL GROWTH, 143; THE PLAN AND
FOREIGN TRADE, 147; HOW DEMOCRATIC IS FRENCH
PLANNING? 149; PARLIAMENT AND THE PLAN, 149;
EFFECT OF THE PLAN ON FRENCH BUREAUCRACY, 152.

7. French regional planning *page* 154

INVOLVING THE NATION, 154; MEDIUM TERM REG-
IONALIZATION, 155; REGIONAL ORGANIZATION, 155;
FINANCIAL STRUCTURE, 156; PUBLIC INVESTMENT, 157;
PROSPECTIVE REMODELLING 161; LOCATION OF INDUS-
TRY, ETC., 161; RESPONSIBILITY, 161; TYPES OF MODELS,
162; REGIONAL METROPOLISES, 164; FRENCH AGRICUL-
TURE, 167.

Index *page* 173

I

Concepts and Definitions

'Ici on devrait peut-être faire quelques remarques sur l'espace,
mot qui change de sens avec la manière de voir et de penser.
L'espace de la pratique ordinaire n'est pas tout à fait le même
que celui du géomètre car ne sont pas toutes les mêmes expéri-
ences ou opérations qui les définissent.'
    Paul Valéry, *Introduction à la méthode de Léonard de Vinci*

¶Implicit in the study of regional planning is the concept of   *Concepts of space*
economic space. The establishment of common markets;
changes in zones of influence; conflict of policies of territorial
remodelling: these are not merely controversial topics; they
invoke questions affecting prosperity and the development of
national space.

Geographers, economists, sociologists, mathematicians, and
businessmen often hold different ideas about space because, as
Valéry pointed out, the significance of space changes with, and is
determined by, the experiences and operations which give birth
to its definition. Space has also an emotive connotation. It is the
traditional *environment* of human existence; it has to do with
acknowledged *rules* and techniques of our activities; sometimes
it is even the ultimate *objective* of the game. Thus as environment, as rules, and as objective, space confronts us, historically
and logically, with a triple notion.

Space was first conceived geographically, as the *blut und boden*
of Geopolitics; the realm of ideas, as formulated by Mackinder.

A

Next, the concept of economic space appeared as a less emotive and more 'operational' notion. Indeed, investment capital, transportation networks, industry, agricultural techniques, create a new theatre with new materials and new rules. Thus economic and geographic conceptions of space are in contra-distinction one to the other. The geographer places man in a so-called natural environment; the economist places environment in the tool-box of human activities. Geographic space is a three-dimensional space confronted with a more complex and multi-dimensional one.

The philosopher might then ask: is economic space not iden-tical with mathematical space? The answer, for two reasons, would be, *no*. First, mathematical space is entirely abstract and has no reference to any geographical location. A good example is given by the economist himself when he speaks of 'indifference surfaces'. If a space were formed solely of economic variables, it would be a mathematical one; it could be anywhere. But economic space, on the contrary, is an application of economic variables on or in a geographical space, through a mathematical transformation which describes an economic process. This can be shown in a simple way:

$$\left[\begin{array}{l}\text{Mathematical Space}\\ \text{(Technical}\\ \text{operator)}\end{array}\right] \underset{\text{applied on}}{} \left[\begin{array}{l}\text{Geographic Space}\\ \text{(Location of}\\ \text{natural resources)}\end{array}\right] \rightarrow \begin{array}{l}\text{Economic Space}\\ \text{(For human use)}\end{array}$$

Homogeneity,
Polarization, and
Finality

¶ This is what happens when industrialists set up and operate a factory, or when administrators decide to build a bridge or a road. These transformations may be considered in three different ways. That is, space can be defined in terms of *homogeneity, polarization, or finality*,[1] just as, in Aristotle's logic, everything can be defined, firstly by *material* description, secondly by *formal* relations, and thirdly in terms of a *final objective* or source of decision.

The concept of *homogeneous* space is intuitive because it is descriptive. That of *polarization* is associated with the relation-ships constructed by the flows of inputs and outputs character-

[1] For discussion see Meyer: *Regional Economics, A Survey* (American Economic Review, March 1963); and François Perroux: *L'Economie du XXe Siècle* (PUF, 1961).

izing human activity: it is more abstract. The teleological concept of *programming* space is created by the goals of man: it is political. But before studying these three concepts more closely, we must make an important distinction between *Space* and *Region*.

¶ Space and region are not synonymous terms. An Economic Region is a continuous and localized area; an Economic Space is not. The group of factories of a large corporation forms a space, but not necessarily a region. The class of French *Departements* (pp. 4,5) with high income *per capita* forms a space, but is not grouped into one contiguous region. For example, Lille (Nord) and Marseilles (Bouches du Rhône) have about the same high income *per capita*, but the poorer *departements* in between prevent contiguity. Thus, if these two *departements* are part of the same homogeneous economic space, they do not belong to a homogeneous economic region, as can be seen from Map 2.

Space and Region

This is not a characteristic of economics only. The orders of mammals, batrachians, birds, and reptiles form a class of vertebrates. But to effect the subdivision of French territory into 'homogeneous vertebrate regions' it is necessary (a) to calculate the density of vertebrata per square kilometre, i.e. to localize the vertebrata set by an application on French soil; (b) to group the data into regions formed of units with an approximately equal density of population. The procedure may be summarized in a simple scheme:

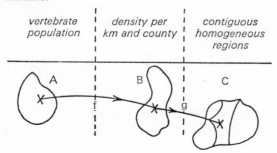

Note 1 : C is an image of B and A, and is a set of regions.
Note 2 : It is possible to compose both relations f and g.

MAP 1

THE *DEPARTEMENTS* OF FRANCE

4

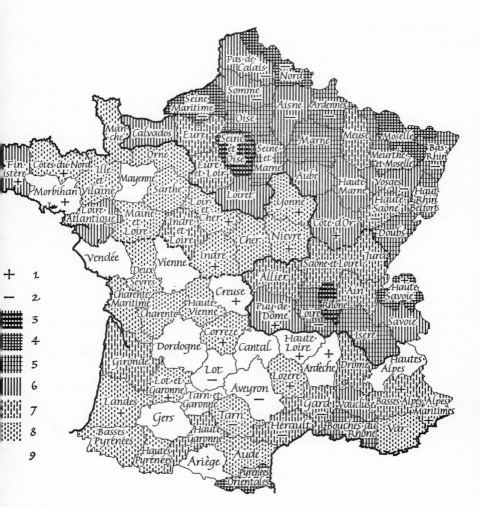

MAP 2

FRENCH HOMOGENEOUS REGIONS

The map shows average income per capita, 1955/6
1 : increase of +5% since 1951   2 : decrease of +5%   3 : average, 120   4 : average
108 to 120   5 : average 96 to 108   6 ; average 88 to 96   7 : average 80 to 88   8 : average
70 to 80   9 : average less than 70.   Extreme positions : Seine, 167 : Lot, 55

Macro and
Micro-economics

¶There is another problem which we must elucidate before studying the concepts of homogeneity, polarization, and programming further. It concerns the difference between macro- and micro-economics. Of course, it is not principally a question of size. Imperial Chemical Industries, with a hundred plants in the UK and fifty subsidiaries overseas, is larger, in some senses, than Mauritius. The distinction is that we deal with *macro-economics* when we speak of group phenomena, populations, measurable sets. Indeed, there is no difference between the statistical notion of population and the mathematical concept of set. Moreover, the set must be larger than one. We deal with *micro-economics* when we study a unique object. The individual consumer or the individual firm may be conceived as unities having no influence whatsoever on one another, and confronted with a given market.[2] This is the orthodox micro-economic concept of partial equilibrium. In this study, our viewpoint is different. We shall deal with spaces and regions forming sets larger than one, and where every element is interconnected with the other ones. This is a general equilibrium approach. When every element is taken explicitly into account, it may be called a micro global study. When some of the relations are partially solved to bring out aggregated concepts such as income, we deal with macro-economics.

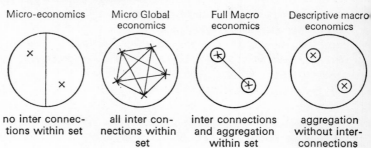

Micro-economics	Micro Global economics	Full Macro economics	Descriptive macro economics
no inter connec-tions within set	all inter con-nections within set	inter connections and aggregation within set	aggregation without inter-connections within set

The concepts of economic space and region are, as we said, the result of applying algebraic or geometric operators on geographic space. But on unprepared soil our sophisticated ploughs

[2] The market cannot be considered as a macro-economic space from the homogeneity point of view, only a set of markets can.

would easily break down. To be able to work usefully, it is necessary to possess two bulldozers, which can trace out rectangular fine tracks; in other words, to construct a double entry table which will, at the start, allow us to give a few examples.

Horizontally, we will employ the three notions of homogeneous space, polarized space, and programming space.

Vertically, we will distinguish between micro- and macroanalysis.

description	micro-economics	macro-economics
homogeneous space or region	e.g. present and potential markets of the enterprise	e.g. study of regional disposable labour
polarized space or region	e.g. study of relations between the main enterprise and its subsidiaries	e.g. regions under the influence of the different regional metropoles
programming space or region	e.g. general linear programming of the enterprise	e.g. river basins development

¶ The homogeneity concept is both the most traditional and the simplest notion. It is well known to geographers, demographers, and economists that a homogeneous region corresponds to a continuous space of which each unit (or constituting zone) has characteristics as proximate as possible to the characteristics of the next unit. *Homogeneity*

A territorial market may be subdivided into zones with differing *per capita* purchasing power. Adjacent zones with high income will form homogeneous regions; zones with a lower purchasing power can be grouped in other homogeneous regions, and poor zones can also be grouped in contiguous units.

More generally, homogeneity is linked with the analytical definition of a *set* in terms of some characteristic which describes each element (e.g. income *per capita*). To increase the utility of the concept, it is necessary to synthetize the population by a central value, and a measure of the degree of dispersion around it. The notion of homogeneity implies the minimization of dispersion. Homogeneous region or space is a macro-economic concept but no economic interdependence appears between its elements. It is purely descriptive.

Moreover, to define homogeneous *spaces*, it is necessary to decide their number arbitrarily beforehand. To take an example; it is necessary to break down national space into an arbitrary number of technical sectors. Ten, twenty, or a hundred homogeneous sectors may be defined in the economy, depending on the problems to be analyzed, on the cost involved, and on the number of skilled analyses available.

Homogeneous regions ¶ Homogeneous *regions* involve another constraint besides that of a predetermined number: the constraint of contiguity. There must not be any geographical gap between the different units of a region. The problem, then, is to minimize dispersion or statistical distance between local characteristics, given two conditions, contiguity and the number of regions. The justification of the notion of contiguity is empirical. Contiguous or adjacent spaces (i.e. neighbours) have more characteristics in common than have stochastic spaces, i.e. geographic zones taken at random. This is a global phenomenon subject to few exceptions. If it were not true, the concept of region would be useless.

To bring out once more the difference between the notion of space and that of region, let us consider the set, or population, of 89 French *departements* and describe their evolution from 1860 to 1960. We will find three great homogeneous regions. First, there is *the most highly developed* (Paris, Paris region, North and East) which, during the nineteenth century, exploited industrially its mineral resources. The resultant industrial prosperity increased the basic wealth derived from the agricultural exploitations of soil and climate. The complementary character of these activities induced an important demographic concentration. This zone is presently growing obsolescent and needs modernization. It is a geographically continuous set. But if we looked, throughout France, for local units presenting similar characteristics, we would find quite a number of them: le Creusot, Saint-Etienne, Mazamet, Saint-Nazaire, for example.

They pertain to the same homogeneous economic space: but not being contiguous to the previous units, they belong to different homogeneous economic regions. The second homogeneous region is *the newly developing zone* (Lyon region and Provence) which benefits from its geographical location on the north-south axis formed by the Rhine, Saône, Rhône valleys and their orientation towards the North African market and natural resources. Improvements in transportation make it possible to switch agriculture and agricultural manpower into new products and industries fitted to a developing Europe with an increasing purchasing power. At the same time, tourism takes advantage of rapid national income growth. The main problem is that of urbanization. This region includes le Creusot and Saint-Etienne as depressed areas.

A third homogeneous region is formed by *less developed and slowly growing regions* of West, South-West and Central France. Its agriculture, which often remains autarchic and has low productivity, accounted for as much as 65 per cent of regional employment in 1962. Towns are less industrial than in other regions, of small size and small attraction. The main problem is that of industrialization. This region includes Bordeaux and Saint-Nazaire as industrialized poles.

We must remember that, even if the homogeneous region includes a contiguity constraint, it is simply a description and classification of economic characteristics of different spatial units. It does not take account of economic relations between its elements or with elements of other regions. At most, it helps to discover correlations between them. Through these relations we are brought to a second notion, the more important because it takes into account economic processes and flows: the concept of polarization.

¶Although the notion of *polarization* is very recent, it is already in common use among geographers, economists, and mathematicians. The study of the hierarchy of cities, towns, and villages; the structural analysis of poles of development in regions of expanding economy; network and graph analysis: these, while barely a quarter of a century old, have all become classical.

Polarization

The polarized region or space provides a description of the relations between its component parts, or with elements of other sets. It enables one to define, formally, interdependent and polarized groups, each with an internal hierarchy.

Interdependence can be described technically, by means of a credit and debit account, an input-output table, or a network of *flows*. Each of these equivalent techniques reveals connections. To represent a space, each account, each row and column, each node of the network has to be localized; to represent a region, the zones of influence they synthetize have to be contiguous.

Polarization involves the notion of *hierarchy*, which is best studied by means of graph analysis. This hierarchy is analogous to that of a national metropolis vis-à-vis a regional capital, the local towns, the small centres and the villages. But the important point concerns the stability of connections and their relative importance.

The polarization concept would be of no practical value unless the interdependencies and hierarchy which it discovers were the expression of stable relations. Thus we are led from the notion of an input-output table to that of a matrix of import or export parameters.[3]

Hierarchy of
Cities
¶ The concept of the polarized region is the offspring of observation of the structure of cities. It is instinctive to visualize a system and hierarchy of communities from metropolis down to village. Every major city has a radius of satellite towns which in turn possess satellite villages. This phenomenon is of the utmost importance in an industrial and commercial civilization where urban growth increases at a rapid pace.

Thus interdependent buying and selling seem characteristic of a set of regional towns contained within a larger set: the nation. A polarized region has been defined as the set of neighbouring towns exchanging more with the regional metropolis than with other cities of the same order in the nation. The justi-

[3] This parametric conception of polarization poses the problem of *aggregation* in a new and complex way. As soon as we have relations, the concepts of summation and mean are not sufficient. It is the notion of equivalent or rather congruent transformation which is the proper one. This is why the degree of matrix aggregation changes the results when studying interdependence problems. Thus a coherent degree of aggregation is absolutely necessary when studying inter-regional problems.

fication of this notion of region is, once more, empirical. *Neigh-bourhood* gives a greater strength to ties of information and relationship. Of course, such ties do not exclude others with different centres. The polarized region is integrated; it is not an autarchy.

For example, the *Region Lyonnaise* – as observed through the intensity of road traffic on national highways – appears to be neatly polarized (see Map 3). The index of absolute increment of traffic (which is more significant and dynamic than a simple intensity map) builds a bridge between the concept of the polarized region and the notion of growth-poles, which is one of the keys to the problem of regional development. A regional growth-pole is a set of expanding industries located in an urban area and inducing further development of economic activity throughout its zone of influence.

¶Another illustration of the interest and significance of the polarization concept is provided by the study of the movement of boundaries connected with the evolution of towns. (Map 4). *Boundary movement of towns*

The best examples can be found in regions where the process of urbanization is fastest, such as in Latin America. Rio Grande do Sul of Brazil offers a specially good instance. Comparison of the zones of influence of the towns in this State, at two successive points in time, shows (1) the impact of the opening of new roads; (2) the influence of demographic growth within the different towns; and (3) the effect of the structural development and differentiation of the towns. Such, for instance, is the lesson of the rivalry between the towns Porto Alegre and Pelotas. In 1954, road traffic showed that the State of Rio Grande do Sul was divided into four regions headed by Porto Alegre, Pelotas, Uruguayana and Passo Fundo. In 1963, as a result of new road construction, we observe a great shift of influence. That of Pelotas is much reduced. That of Porto Alegre increases in the south and west, tending to absorb a part of the Pelotas and Passo Fundo regions. Only that of Uruguayana remains the same. The reasons behind this change of regional boundaries are of interest and deserve further attention.

First, the lack of communication forced upon Pelotas has, for twenty years, enabled Porto Alegre to grow faster than its old rival.

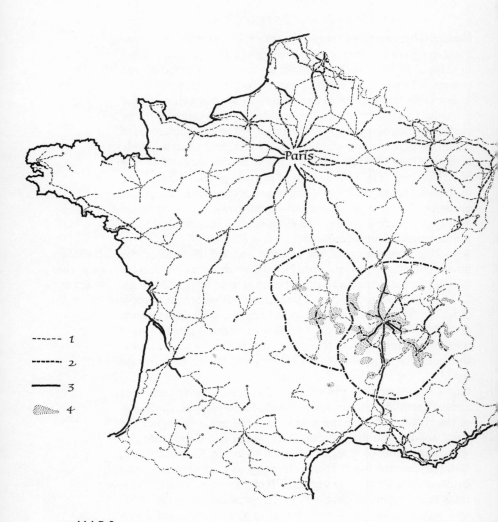

MAP 3

POLARIZED REGIONS OF LYON AND CLERMONT

as shown by traffic intensity. Daily averages of general Traffic increases on routes nation ales. 1 : 750-1000 2 : 1001-2000 3 : above 2000 4 : urban and industrial areas

MAP 4

RIO GRANDE DO SOL, BRAZIL

showing the polarized region of Porto Alegre, based on traffic intensity. 2 :Polarized region of Porto Alegre in 1954. 1 : Extension of Porto Alegre region, 1954-63

Secondly, in 1960, when Porto Alegre was large enough (618,000 inhabitants compared with 125,000 for Pelotas) a highway was opened between the two towns and Reilly's Law (see p. 30) then operated in favour of Porto Alegre, pushing back the Pelotas region up to the Rio Camagua.

Thirdly, this situation, at present favourable to the State capital, will change again to one of national weakness when confronted with the influence of the larger Uruguayan city of Montevideo, through the opening of the Latin American Common Market (ALALC).

Until now, we have defined and, to a large extent, contrasted the notions of homogeneous and polarized space and regions. They do not, however, compete with one another, and are complementary. A polarized region is formed of heterogeneous units. It is true that every economic space can be visualized either as a set of units more or less similar to one another or as a set of nodes related one to another. But a space or region of maximum homogeneity is different from a space or region of maximum interconnection.

In France the urbanized industrial regions form patches (which add up to a homogeneous space). But these poles are linked with one another by traffic flows. This transport network shapes polarized regions. Adjacent cities, such as Lyon and Clermont Ferrand, naturally seem to belong to the same homogeneous region, but the low volume and relative unimportance of connecting road traffic indicate that the economic life of the two towns is entirely distinct.

PROSPECTIVE AND PROGRAMMING

¶ From the regional as well as from the national point of view, the second part of the twentieth century is characterized by *prospective* philosophy. *Prospective* is a policy, in contrast to a forecast, which is merely a projection. Science today is not simply an effort of unbiased description and impartial forecast. It is also a tool, a way to achieve a goal in the most economic way. 'The day before yesterday men followed *unconsciously* what we call Nature. Yesterday men complied with nature carefully and candidly. Today our power of action has developed in such a way that we need no longer rely on regulations external to our own deeds. It belongs to us at times to protect nature, at times to set it on more favourable ways. We are in a sense responsible for evolution' (Gaston Berger).[4]

In France, as in Great Britain, public opinion is now sufficiently well-informed to distinguish between *forecast* and *prospective* – two technical and most helpful concepts. Scientifically, a *prevision* or forecast is the projection of a trend, whether we have an isolated variable or the extrapolation of many variables linked through a model. The hypothesis concerning the exogenous variables enables us to reach specific conclusions. Thus economic forecasting may reveal, for example, dangerous possibilities (unemployment or inflation) which should be fought and prevented. But this plain attitude is very different from prospective, which is a policy from the start, or what is called, in jargon, a teleological concept. Prospective does not aim at smoothing forecasted and spontaneous cyclical fluctuations or forecasted inflation. It aims at establishing an objective that no spontaneous trend indicates as probable, and at determining the ways and means necessary to reach this objective with balanced growth.

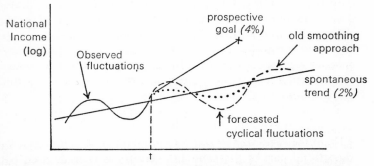

This is not just an extension of the traditional forecasting problem and of the smoothing of fluctuation. The objective (4 per cent on the graph) is not a constraint in the initial cyclical model. Prospective gives birth to a *voluntary modification* of economic structure which is in no way spontaneous. It suppresses the bottlenecks and goes far beyond the long-term view.

[4] Prospective No. 1, PUF 1948.

This is why prospective models include various instruments of policy, and generate decisions. In short, a prospective or decision model is built of three blocks and can be illustrated as follows:

$$\begin{bmatrix} \text{Matrix of the} \\ \text{economic} \\ \text{structure} \end{bmatrix} \times \begin{bmatrix} \text{Vector of the} \\ \text{policy} \\ \text{instruments} \end{bmatrix} = \begin{bmatrix} \text{Vector of} \\ \text{final} \\ \text{objectives} \end{bmatrix}$$

To be true, the vector of final objectives has to be decided upon in advance, in order that the set of policies and instruments may be calculated. This introduces further complicated and organic problems in the programming of space and region.

Programming
Space and Region
¶The *programming space* is defined in terms of the coherence or unity of economic decisions. A unique and rational decision-maker is only a limiting case, seldom found in practice: more commonly, decisions are made by a diverse group of decentralized organizations. The French planning experience has so far shown that national or regional programming space is not beyond achievement in a free economy. All decision centres agree to the same finality or 'concerted decisions' as indicated in the *Plan*. There is no need for dictatorial enforcement: a moral pledge has been shown to be sufficient. Thus, on the national or regional level the *programming space* is a tool in the hands of the national and regional authorities in order to reach a given objective. It is built on sectoral localized analysis. It is a geographically discontinuous, and an economically functional, instrument.

The *programming region* is a geographically continuous tool. However, the localization of the decision centre within the region is not essential. It may be in London or in Edinburgh, in Paris or in Lyon. This is why the problems of co-ordination and decentralization arise. The two extreme solutions are the Federal States in the United States and the twenty-one programming regions in France. In France a simple co-ordination of different administrative units forming a number of *departements* and the polarization of economic activities traces out a new administrative map (No. 5). This map is close to a polarization map because the maximum efficiency in regional program-

MAP 5
THE FRENCH PROGRAMMING REGIONS
(Medium-Term, 4-5 Year Planning)

17

ming is linked with the maximum interconnection of regional flows.

A correlation exists between the length of the Plan and the size of the programming region. For traditional year-to-year current administration the *departement* is large enough; for medium-term (four year) plans the larger twenty-one programming regions are necessary; for long-term (fifteen to twenty years) prospective development three to eight remodelling regions only should be taken into account (*régions d'aménagement du territoire*).

Within these limits two categories of problems arise. First, the choice of instruments of policy. Secondly, the choice of objectives.

Choice of Instruments ¶ Let us first assume that the objectives are chosen. Then programming is the determination of the effectiveness of the economic instruments chosen, to enable a region to reach a given objective in a given period of time. The given objective may be one or a set of several aims. For example: (a) *Welfare*: the maximum rate of growth of regional income; (b) *Power*: enlarging or reinforcing the geographic regional influence through a dynamic border policy; (c) *Equality:* equalization of regional and/or group income *per capita*.

To attain these objectives the economic tools are numerous and interdependent and include the following. (1) The *choice* of a growth sector in a given region. (2) The *localization* of a propulsive industry or university. Let us take examples in Scotland. Is the Grangemouth/Falkirk area well chosen to increase its population by as much as 30,000? Will Grangemouth/Falkirk be situated in the polarized economic zone of Edinburgh or of Glasgow and on which town will it have its greatest indirect impact? With the opening of new communications, what will be the economic influence zones of a 55,000 population in Glenrothes, and a 80,000 population in Cumbernauld? (3) The creation of new energy resources. (4) The determination of local levels of salaries, taxes, and credit. (What are the actual wage levels in the new town zones, what impact will pilot industries' location have?) (5) Any other strategic and localized instrument aimed at maximizing the regional economic activity.

As may be seen, none of these tools can be appropriated to a single object, as every one of them has various indirect impacts. Conversely, the interconnection of activities makes it necessary to build a co-ordinating regional authority, e.g. the Scottish Development Group, the French Préfet Regional, and the Regional Development Commission. The specific project-procedure, with the estimation of gains and costs, has to be co-ordinated with priorities of developmental planning. These in turn have to be introduced as a development of more global national harmonization figures obtained from linear programming models, which should become the major economic tools of advanced countries.

¶ Since each specific plan is characterized by its aims, the programming region raises the problem of *hierarchy between regional and national objectives*. These are not spontaneously consistent; for instance, the maximization of national and regional incomes. If the objective were to maximize, in a given period, the income of each region, national growth might be slowed down to a considerable extent. National resources are always limited, regional productivities are unequal, and regional interconnections different. Investment in the less productive, less well-endowed regions would put a brake on the development of more productive ones. Investment in regions less closely linked with the economic core of the nation than others, would make a lower impact on total growth. Conversely, it is socially unacceptable to invest in the expanding and richest regions only. Thus, every time choice has to be made of a set of final goods, problems of social and political welfare are bound to arise.

Regional and National Hierarchy

At present, and for the sake of illustration, it would be helpful to sketch a very simple solution to the problem of regional and national hierarchy.

Let us admit that the main objective of national regional policy is the enrichment of the community with, as a necessary constraint, the relative improvement of the poorer group.

With these premises we have defined our problem: how to maximize the sum of regional incomes without any poor regions' growth being inferior to the mean rate. It can be solved through linear programming or simple approximation.

Let us take four regions, the weight of which, in terms of income, are a_1, a_2, a_3, a_4, let their growth rate be p_1, p_2, p_3, p_4, and admit that a_1, the richest region, has the fastest growth rate p_1, and so on. Of course, if the fourth region is the poorest, its rate of growth is inferior to the average national rate p and we want it to be at least equal $(p_4 \geqslant p)$ with $p = a_1 p_1 + a_2 p_2 + a_3 p_3 + a_4 p_4$ maximum. Thus the constraint may be written down as $a_1 p_1 + a_2 p_2 + a_3 p_3 + (a_1 - 1) p_4 \leqslant 0$. This is nothing else but a linear programming model.

But to be simple in this introduction, let us consider only a rough-and-ready approximation to the general solution, based on the Brazilian experience. Let the four regions be (1) the richest part of Brazil: Rio-Guanabara-São Paulo; (2) the second richest: Rio Grande do Sul-Parana-Santa Catarina; (3) we find just under the federal mean: Minas-Espirito Santo; (4) the desolated regions of the north and north-east.

From 1950 to 1960 the development of these four regions was influenced by the impact of the Sudene Plan[5] which induced the economic take-off of the north-east between 1955 and 1960; during the same period we observe the relative decline of Minas Gerais.

This situation can be improved, as may be shown in the following example, where Brazilian growth is kept at the rate of 4 per cent, and the growth of north-east at 5 per cent, in order to realize a relative improvement of the poorer region. All necessary indications are shown on Table No. 1.[6]

TABLE 1

	region	weight (% of GNP)		growth rate		weighted growth
4	North-east, North	0·2	×	5%	=	1
3	Minas-Espirito Santo	0·1	×	4%	=	0·4
2	South	0·2	×	5%	=	1
1	Rio-Guanabara-São Paulo	0·5	×	(3·2)%	=	(1·6)
	Brazil	1·0		4%		4%

[5] Under the impulsion of Celso Furtado.
[6] To get the *per capita* growth one would have only to deduct demographic growth from income growth.

The figures in brackets in columns 2 and 3 are easy to determine. Total national growth is formed of regional weighted growth adding up to 4 per cent. The missing figure is thus 1·6 in the last column. The growth rate of region 1 is 3·2 in the second column. Note that in this solution the poorer regions do not grow at a slower pace than the national mean, and that the south resumes its role of development pole, owing to a very small decline of the richest region's rate from 3·6 to 3·2. Due to the weight of Rio-Guanabara-São Paulo (50 per cent), this small decline is quite sufficient. This is a very general phenomenon. Each time the richest region concedes a small fraction of its 'large' share of net investment, it is possible to assist, to a large extent, the rate of growth of the poorer regions. The only problem appears to be that of *national productivity*.

Due to heavier social costs in the richest region (possessing the largest metropolis), and due to the market imperfections, it is not certain that the location of enterprises should be decided by profit motive alone.

Note that the same relative improvement of the poorest can be studied also in terms of personal income brackets. In France the SMIG, or minimum salary level, is geared to the cost of living, so that the purchasing power will remain constant.

However, with a 5·5 rate of growth of the national product and a population increase of 0·8 per annum, the *per capita* income growth is 4·7 per cent. It would, therefore, be desirable to avoid a relative decline in the lowest income brackets, by gearing it to this national *per capita* growth rate.

Regional and social improvement of the poorest regions are linked through the agricultural problem. The rural areas have the slowest growth rates, with the result that the peasants are the real proletariat of today. Thus in developed countries a solution to this problem could be found through the agricultural technique complex. In the developing countries the solution depends on the new industrial base. In both stages of development, it is imperative to possess a sufficient number of technical experts, and to provide them with statistical data, and the instruments of economic and financial policy.

The Tools for Regional Economic Studies

Empirical Foundations ¶ The results of any work are greatly conditioned by the tools used, and the value of an intellectual tool or of an economic concept must be judged largely by results and not by *a priori* reasoning. This is why we attach great importance to the tools which give reality and existence to the abstract notions of homogeneity, polarization, and programming. Indeed, these notions are inherently linked to the operational work achieved through them. Problems of definition would be largely a waste of time and a mere scholastic temptation, if they did not help to solve problems of regional economic policy.

To what extent is our basic and logical distinction successful? What is the empirical meaning of our three notions?[1]

Basically, the answer is simple. The foundation of spatial and regional notions consists of economic data, and the final aim is action in favour of Man.

1. To achieve our goal we have, first, to obtain local information adequate to give existence to our explicative scheme, and to differentiate regions from the point of view of homogeneity and polarization. In practice this means finding out, among other things, the demographic composition of the region, the breakdown of the labour force by industry or sector, the local cost-of-living level, and the size of regional income. The last two are

[1] Cf. John Meyer: *Regional Economics, A Survey* (American Economic Review, March 1963).

more difficult to obtain and more often than not remain un-
known.

This type of approach may be synthetized in a very simple
diagram.

2. Secondly, we have to determine the regional mechanism of
goal setting and the geographical technique for maximizing
the chosen goals. However, in the present chapter we shall
limit outselves to the study of the statistical and economic
instruments which permit us to observe homogeneous or
polarized regions, and to fix their boundaries. Later we shall
study the complex problem of the programming region.

OBSERVATIONAL METHODS

¶Every regional statistical programme has to deal both with
the classification of local economic data and with local economic
relations between factors or agents of production. The sets of
descriptive data – e.g. production, consumption, labour forces
– define homogeneous regions. The relations – e.g. trade
between two towns, traffic circulation, financial flows – link

different poles and help to define the polarized regions. These relations suppose at least *two* entities, *two* double-entry accounts, *two* nodes on a graph. Note also that polarized regions may not exist in the autarchic economies of underdeveloped countries. In these countries the programming region which aims at creating development poles – e.g. on the Orinoco valley – precedes the existence of the polarized regions themselves. The opposite is true in respect of the 'new towns' in Scotland, which fit into a network of existing polarized regions. On the other hand, homogeneous regions can always be studied, whatever the degree of development of the country. Thus the homogeneous region appears to be a more general concept. It is also the simplest.

Homogeneity ¶An economic space or region is never perfectly homogeneous.
Analysis Regional statistics, from the point of view of homogeneity, help us to analyse dispersion (space) and contiguity (region).

(*a*) The *classical dispersion analysis* is made through the computation of mean and standard deviation. The intention of such a method is to individualize new synthetic units by common and stable characteristics. Moreover, interspatial comparison is a good substitute for intertemporal comparison in correlation research. Regional homogeneous characteristics may also be thought of as a goal when choosing political objectives and political means, e.g. income *per capita*, low level of unemployment, localization of technical schools, etc.

But this type of analysis has limits to its accuracy. Observed units must not be too small. Even with complete statistical information, calculation of a birth rate in a town is subject to stochastic fluctuations through time and has a 95 per cent chance of being in between

$$p \pm 2\sqrt{\frac{p(1-p)}{n}}$$

where n is the population and p is the mean rate of birth. Thus n has to be great, if we want a sufficient approximation. The same reasoning applies to stochastic samples of a stable economic phenomenon observed in a region. In this case, the region has to be large enough.[2] This is why there are no more than

[2] Gabriel Chevry: *La Statistique Régionale Interêt et Limites* (Congrès de Quitandinha, Brazil 1955).

twenty-one statistical regions in France. This has become, to a large extent, classical.

(b) *Contiguity analysis* is more recent and far more interesting. Contiguity is the condition differentiating space units and region units. It is an empirical notion. Unit-zones, geographically close to each other, are more likely to possess common characteristics than units picked at random from an economic space. This is, in fact, the justification of the empirical notion of the homogeneous region.

To demonstrate and measure the influence of contiguity or regionalism we may proceed in three steps, which technically improve one on another.

(1) Let us take two samples: the first, of one hundred pairs of adjacent counties; the second, of one hundred pairs of counties drawn at random. We consider income *per capita* as the characteristic to be studied in each county. We compute in two different columns the squares of the income differences between each pair of adjacent and each pair of random counties. We make a summation for each column and we find that the total of differences between adjacent counties is the smaller figure of the two. These sums are, in fact, equal to double the variance in each set. We conclude that contiguous counties are economically more like one another than counties taken at random. The contiguity or regional effect becomes evident.

(2) We could also take *n* counties of a given region and a sample of *n* counties taken at random in the national space. In order to be closer to classical dispersion analysis, we could compute the variance of the two sets. The variance of the contiguous counties would be much smaller than that of the stochastic ones.

(3) Taking the matter further, R. C. Geary[3] gives a quantitative measure of the influence of contiguity for a given set of neighbouring geographical units. He computes a ratio between the variance of the chosen characteristic in neighbouring counties and the variances in the total population.

In fact, Geary writes the numerator as the sum of squared

[3] R. C. Geary: *The Contiguity Ratio* (The Incorporated Statistician, 1954).

differences of pairs of neighbouring units, which amounts to the double of the variance. If the characteristic is income (R), we have the combination $\sum_i \sum_{i'}{}^\star (R_i - R_i')$, which is equal to the double of total squared deviation from the mean income.

We have only to divide by the total number of contiguous units to obtain the double of the variance. This means that the variance is:

$$\frac{1}{2} \frac{1}{\sum_i k_{i'}} \sum_i \sum_{i'}{}^\star (R_i - R_i')^2$$

$\sum^\star$ = summation of contiguous units. $\sum_i k_{i'}$ = number of contiguous units to i'. The denominator of Geary's ratio is the ordinary variance of the population :

$$\frac{1}{n} \sum_i (R_i - R)^2 \quad R = \text{mean of sample.}$$

The contiguity ratio is thus:

$$C = \frac{1}{2} \cdot \frac{\dfrac{1}{\sum_i K_{i'}} \sum_i \sum_{i'}{}^\star (R_i - R_i')^2}{\dfrac{1}{n} \sum_i (R_i - R)^2}$$

The influence of contiguity is thus measured by the ratio of dispersions between characteristics of contiguous and random units. The Geary coefficient appears to be an improvement on the first method described above. It gives a measure of the regional effect that we had put in evidence.

Correlation Analysis ¶ Two other paths to the measure of contiguity can be found in correlation analysis between two or more variables. The regional effect may be thought of as a residual factor or as a cause of local differences between the regression coefficients.

As an example, consider, with Duncan,[4] the salaries of textile workers. The study of regional income as a regional characteristic in the United States tells us that low textile salaries are linked with the industry's main location in the south. This is a statement identical to that of Molière's doctor: 'And this is why your daughter is dumb'. It does not explain *why* salaries are low

[4] O. D. Duncan and Duncan: *Statistical Geography* (Free Press of Glencoe, Illinois).

in the south. It is a pure description, not a measure of regional effect. We have to turn to an analysis of the low salaries in the south and find correlations between different levels of salaries and independent variables, such as the structure of industry, the cost of living, syndicalism, etc. After having eliminated every casual influence, a true regional effect would appear as the remaining and unaccounted part.

There is, however, another manifestation of regional influence. The regression coefficients between the wages and the independent variables (industrial structure, cost of living, etc.) differ, over a period, from region to region. So also with household consumption and family income. This is a manifestation of regional character.

Correlation and regression coefficients will change with the outline of the boundaries of the region. How should we proceed, in order to get the best correlation possible and the largest differentiation between regression coefficients? There is no logical method beyond successive approximation, but it does allow us to determine the homogeneous region.

¶ The originality of the concepts of polarized space and region lies in the fact that both are more than a total description of separate poles or economic entities. They give an account of the connections *between* centres of production, consumption, and distribution. A good example of the difference between homogeneous and polarized regions maybe found in the map of industrial and urban population established for France by Le Filatre; and the picture given by road circulation from town to town (Map No. 3). The first map (to be found on page 59) is that of a homogeneous and discontinuous space, that of French agglomerations and industrial zones. The second map reveals, through traffic flows, the texture of contiguous polarized regions, the poles of which appear on the first image. The super-imposition of the two maps would provide illuminating evidence about the Rhône-Alpes and Auvergne regions. They seem almost to form a homogeneous economic unit on the first map and appear to be isolated from one another on the second. These maps illustrate the fact that the maximum of homogeneity and the maximum interconnection of economic entities are two different

Polarization Analysis

notions, although this fact has sometimes been questioned.[5]

We will slip over the exhaustive and ponderous description of the flows existing in a polarized region.[6] In any event, it rests on the assumption that the hierarchy between the poles has been predetermined. This is why I shall first indicate a technique for describing regional relationships and determining regional hierarchy.

Formal description   ¶Although urban hierarchy is an empirical phenomenon, it is connected with the logical or mathematical analysis of inter-relationship, and stresses the difference between the discontinuous space and the continuous region.

Economic flows can always be represented in three ways: through traditional accounting methods, through a double-entry table, and through graph analysis.

Let us illustrate this, using the example of total trade flows between the six countries of the European Community during 1962. Here we have six economic nodes, and $\frac{n(n-1)}{2}$ flows between them, as shown in the following double-entry table.

TABLE 1
External trade between the six countries of the EEC, 1962

(Millions of $)

	1 France	2 Belgium Luxembourg	3 Netherlands	4 Germany	5 Italy	CEE
1	—	660	251	1·319	535	2·764
2	497	—	1051	691	166	2·405
3	288	671	—	1·051	163	2·174
4	1·324	850	1·235	—	1·024	4·432
5	414	134	147	935	—	1·630
CEE	2·523	2·315	2·683	3·996	1·888	13·405

Source: *Statistiques de base de la communauté*

[5] Cf. Meyer: *Regional Economics* (American Economic Review, March 1963).
[6] Cf. Cahiers de l'ISEA, Serie L No. 3—*L'Economie Régionale, Espace Operationnel*, June 1958.

As yet no hierarchy has been established. To understand the economic meaning of the following graph analysis we must remind ourselves of the definition of a *polarized space*. A polarized space could be defined as the set of spatial units conveying, with one of them (called the dominant pole), larger flows than with other poles of the same order. Thus we have most often to make use of a quantitative matrix and a weighted associated graph, in order to compare the flows and retain only the largest of them. It could, it is true, suffice that we should be able to classify them through their relative importance; or, in technical terms, to order them.

However, let us go back to the quantitative matrix of European trade. The polarization principle is to keep for each node or country only the strongest connection with other nodes or countries. Three connections may be of interest: imports, exports, and total trade. Here, for the sake of synthesis, we will retain total trade only, as shown in the following table.

Matrix of total trade†

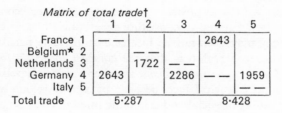

	1	2	3	4	5
France 1	— —			2643	
Belgium★ 2		— —			
Netherlands 3		1722	— —		
Germany 4	2643		2286	— —	1959
Italy 5					— —
Total trade	5·287			8·428	

TABLE 2
Global polarization of EEC through total foreign trade

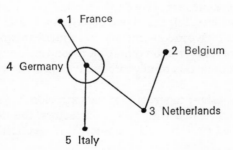

1 France
2 Belgium
4 Germany
3 Netherlands
5 Italy

Source: *Statistiques de base de la communauté* 1964

★ Belgium and Luxembourg are considered as one unity.
† Total trade = imports + exports.

It appears in this table (which should be read column by column) that Germany (4) is the dominant European pole of the six and that Belgium is linked with the Netherlands. Two intuitive notions are thus confirmed. As far as Germany is concerned, she is no satellite of France (with which she has the largest trade flow) because France has a smaller volume of external trade than Germany and thus appears less important from the standpoint of the criterion we have chosen.

Our polarization analysis, then, rests on two lemmata. First, a pole (town, region or country) is said to be independent when its most important flow of activity is oriented towards a less important pole. Secondly, when pole [a] is a satellite of pole [b], and when pole [b] is a satellite of pole [c], pole [a] is also a satellite of pole [c] (transitivity).

From these two lemmata it follows that it is not possible for any pole to be polarized by one of its satellites. A polarization graph is acyclical.

The analysis made for countries is also suitable for towns. In the mathematical polarized space, the towns or economic units are not required to constitute geographically contiguous zones; they may even not be localized at all. The peculiarity of the polarized region is that *the adjacent towns do form a cluster of contiguous urban regions.* In other words, the polarized region is an empirical fact, because proximity is one of the greatest causes of social and economic intercourse. Language, flags, and customs are needed to break this spontaneous pattern.

Tentative Exploratory Research
¶ To be meaningful, the above description has to show some stability. We have to construct models which explain the existing structure of trade and communications, and its future evolution, with the localization of new productive units and new population.

It is important to stress that the extension of the polarized region is correlated with two main factors: the demographic importance of towns, and the internal diversification of their functions.

The demographic importance of towns is a synthetic concept and is related in economic theory with Reilly's law of commercial gravitation. This law states that the commercial flow between two towns is proportional to population size and in inverse proportion of a certain power of the intervening distance between them. We will find that this power is itself a function of the diversification of economic activities in each town.

Urban hierarchy and geographic influence are not determined solely by commercial and tertiary activities (trade, transport, and other services), as German geographers have contended, but also by the diversification of industries. Doubtless, it is well known that small rural centres have simple retail shops and that when they rise in the urban hierarchy there appear other commercial and cultural activities and services: e.g. banks, insurance companies, and universities. But industrialization lies at the heart of the urbanization of the nineteenth and twentieth centuries. Chambers of Commerce have changed to Chambers of Industry, and there is no precise correlation between national or regional income and tertiary employment or value added, as Phyllis Deane and W. Cole have shown in their book on British economic growth.[7]

TABLE 3
Evolution of British tertiary employment (as % of total employed population)

	trade %	public service and professional %	domestic and personal %	total tertiary* %	national income per head at 1913-14 prices £
1891	15	7·	16	38	40
1901	14	11	14	39	47
1911	13	11	14	38	49
1921	13	18	7	38	44
1931	16	18	8	42	49
1951	14	22	2	38	62

* Transport excluded. Source: *op. cit.,* Table 31 and 90.

Thus from 1891 to 1951 national income increased by 50 per cent, while the proportion of trade labour force, in total employment, declined slightly. The authors even show that the size of the total tertiary labour force (trade, personal, public, professional and all other) remained nearly constant (around 38 per

[7] *British Economic Growth 1868-1959: Trends and Structure* (Cambridge University Department of Applied Economics, Monograph 8, Cambridge 1962).

cent). Moreover, the value added by trade done declined from 18 per cent to 16 per cent of national income between 1907 and 1955. We are very far from the tertiary civilization as it is often misinterpreted. The assertion must be understood to mean that the 'white collar' and intellectual workers form a growing part of industrial employment.

Under these circumstances, it is most important to emphasize and differentiate. In fact, we find that small towns specialize in one or two products, whilst large towns have a greater industrial differentiation. Indeed, a regional metropolis is at that level of hierarchy because it disposes of the whole gamut of industrial and commercial activities. Thus polarization is linked with diversification of activities and one of the tools for our study of regional economics will have to be *differentiation coefficients*. Such a differentiation provides a further weighting to the demographic importance of towns. An agricultural town of 10,000 inhabitants, which could be called a traditional eighteenth-century centre, has not the same force of radiation as a diversified industrial agglomeration with a similar population.

Let us stress here that polarization and hierarchy are defined by the dominance of a metropolis over satellites. The *causes* of nodal influence are the size and diversification of the functions of the regional capital. Causes must not be confused with effects.

DETERMINING REGIONAL BOUNDARIES

¶The significance of regional delimitation is illustrated by a well-known feature of American evolution: the disappearance of the frontier. During the second part of the nineteenth century, the United States was divided into the old and industrialized eastern coast and a new and agricultural western region, forming two different homogeneous regions.

The history of American development is one of the swallowing up of the western frontier by the industrialized east through progressive polarization. This was so evident to American minds that a whole economic theory was built, which explained American stagnation between the two wars in terms of the disappearance of the old frontier. Moreover, the Kennedy administration made determined efforts to create a *New Fron-*

tier, not in the geographic sense, as in the nineteenth century, but in the field of economic space – namely in social overhead capital and collective consumption.

Although the American case is a special one, it is true, nevertheless, that every country has problems of expanding or contracting economic regions, and that it has to find the causes of such phenomena. To be able to do this accurately, a preliminary and necessary task is to define the boundaries of the national homogeneous and polarized regions.

¶ The basic principle for tracing boundaries is to group together, and separate in distinct geographic spaces, a number of local units with characteristics as close as possible to one another. These characteristics may be simple and unique, such as income *per capita*, or a complex array of different qualities, such as literacy, standard of industrialization, birth rate, and so on. Therefore, two problems arise, one static and the other dynamic. The static one is how to deal with an array of characteristics, the dynamic one is how to depict the movement of boundaries between different homogeneous regions. *Boundaries of Homogeneous Regions*

¶A region cannot, in fact, be described by a simple trait. And more often than not the different features are incommensurable, e.g. literacy, industrialization, and income *per capita*. *(a) Plurality of Heterogeneous Characteristics*

In order to bring together the regions on a basis of common distinctive traits, we can either construct a 'privileged ordering', which reduces the problem to a continuous single chain of influence, or group all these characteristics in sub-groups, giving to each one a separate chain of influence. This latter method will undoubtedly lead to inconsistencies and value judgments. Moreover, it is most difficult to compare the sizes of each intervening space or chain without being forced upon some 'cardinal' measurement and the laborious problem of weighting, the importance of which is brought out by three fundamental methods for using indices: (i) the fixed index; (ii) the variable index; and (iii) the cluster methods.

(i) *The fixed index* is the simplest method. A number of characteristics (indices) common to regions are chosen, e.g. income *per capita*, unemployment, rate of industrialization. An

C

arbitrary weight is given to each index and a single weighted mean is obtained for each region. Then contiguous regions, with similar indices, are grouped together in order to minimize the variance within each group. Assuming that the weighted mean of a region [y] is closer to the weighted mean of group B than, let us say, to group A, then region [y] belongs to group B. Needless to say, this depends on the weights chosen. Therefore, it is useful to know to what extent a change of weights would alter the grouping. The absence of sensitivity for a reasonable (10 per cent) interval of variation in each weight would indicate a reliable drawing. But we are coming close to the second method.

(ii) *The variable index* method is mostly used in another context, where the variable weights of indices may be chosen to reflect the proportional activities in each region. Suppose that two regions, A and B, both produce wheat, coal and manufactures. The weight given to each activity, in each region, will be different and in accordance with the value or volume regionally produced. If region A is the wheat region, the weight of the wheat index will be the largest, whereas region B, considered to be the coal region, will have a larger weight for the index of coal; and so on. This is a logical method, provided the criteria can be compared to one another; but when one is *literacy* and the other *steel production*, the problem can only be solved through the cluster method.

(iii) *The cluster method* is used to detect the homogeneous character of the structures of different regional units. As an economic structure can be a set of homogeneous flows between different regional sectors and those of other regions, this technique seems to build a bridge between homogeneity and polarization analysis. Nevertheless, the group of regions which forms a homogeneous set will be different from the group of regions which forms a polarized set. Thus the Netherlands and Southern Italy belong to the same polarized set of EEC; but Southern Italy, together with Greece, Turkey, Spain, and North America, form a homogeneous set, of which the Netherlands is not a part. In homogeneity analysis, we look at income and trade flows in themselves, for comparison's sake, and not as links uniting regions and countries.

The general form of the method can be illustrated in the following simple example. We assume three regions $[j, k, l]$ and the rest of the world $[m]$. The transactions which take place between them can be described by two main blocks:

TABLE 4

	Intra-Regional block j		External Block jm		
	Produc- tion	Rest of Economy	Produc- tion	Rest of Economy	
Produc- tion	—	Tjj	Xjm	—	Produc- tion
Rest of Econ.	Vjj	—	Vjm	Ejm	Rest of Econ.

Where Vjj = value added in j;
 Tjj = final goods in j;
 Xjm = exports from j to m;
 Vjm = external income from m to j and
 Ejm = external saving from m to j.

Thus we can obtain a complete balanced matrix. Out of these five transactions, four are independent and describe the region as a dot in a four-dimensional space.

¶Amongst these dotted regions some form a cluster; others are isolated. The cluster is a first approximation to a homogeneous region. Suppose that France has been divided into three regions: the north and east; the west and south-west; and the great Paris region. These form homogeneous sets based on four independent indices; Vjj, Tjj, Xm, and Vm. Each region is represented as one point on a four-dimensional space. By the same reasoning we can extend this to comprehend n dimensional space, provided that we also have n independent characteristics or indices. However, to make this notion clearer, it is necessary to measure the distance between the points as they appear in the n-dimensional space. This distance can be expressed as follows:

(b) Plotting a Homogeneous Region

$$(d_{jk})^2 = \sum_t (x_{tj} - x_{tk})^2 \quad t = 1, 2, \ldots n.$$

where d is the distance between two regions, i.e. j and k, and $t = 1 \ldots n$ transactions or indices.

So far, the analysis has been restricted to describing the *absolute* economic structures between regions. Hence the *relative* importance of each economic magnitude within the region itself has been ignored. And it is the similarity of structure which is important. There are, however, two ways in which to arrive at this. First, we may divide the individual value of transactions in each column by their total value in order to obtain the percentage coefficients which are identical with the Leontief coefficients; and, therefore, their sum total must be equal to one: secondly, by 'normalizing', that is to say, by transforming the matrix so that the sum of the *squared value* of transactions in each column is equal to one. We may then group the regions in clusters, so as to obtain a mean of the square of distances within the cluster smaller than the sum of squared distances between regions. It is worth remembering that this technique enables us to derive a homogeneous space and not a homogeneous region; because we have ignored the contiguity constraint. A region will, therefore, be formed by selecting those points which have a joint boundary with at least one of the other points of the cluster.

(c) Movement of Boundaries

¶The movement of boundaries of homogeneous regions receives a classical illustration with the American frontier problem already alluded to. The frontier region may be defined as a new territory giving increasing returns to labour and capital, for a given technique. In the United States the closing of the frontier was signalized by Alvin Hansen as one of the causes of maturity and stagnation. Of course, this is neither a general nor a sufficient explanation. In underdeveloped countries, the take-off is preceded by stagnation, although an open frontier exists. In developed countries, stagnation is the consequence of maturity even in the absence of any previous frontier. The Kennedy administration tried to show that a 'new frontier' could be opened within the national economic space although the national territory possessed no more virgin regions offering increasing returns.

Thus the problem is twofold. On the one hand, we have the developing countries which have whole areas within their territory sparsely populated, and at a low technical level; in such areas, immigration and modern techniques will rapidly produce increasing returns. This was once the case in the United States; today the absence of land reform prevents its appearance in Brazil. On the other hand, in mature economies such as England, Scotland, and the United States, the frontier assumes a different significance and is used in another context. It consists of sectors, some of which are public, and have a direct, indirect or lateral impact – a propulsive effect on the economy which can be compared with that of the Old Western frontier of the United States. The problem in this case is not regional but spatial. It can be described in a graph or matrix but not on a map. A notable exception to this rule is found on the border of England and Scotland, which has a low density of population, associated with decreasing returns. Therefore, the location of new and propulsive industries could transform it into a frontier. The same could be true for the Highlands of Scotland. This is to anticipate the problem of regional programming which will be the subject matter of the next chapters.

¶ It is important not to confuse a frontier movement with mere migration of industry. The first does not imply a decline in the employment of labour and in the amount of capital which have been utilized to produce the goods and services in the old area. That is why London, Paris, São Paulo, or Central Scotland are not, and cannot be regarded as, frontiers. In fact, a movement into the new frontier area must result in an overall increase of wealth and activity in the old area, and, therefore, in a rise in its demand for labour and capital. As B. Higgins puts it,[8] a frontier exists if the migration of labour and capital causes a rise in the marginal productivity of the mature economy without raising it above the level of the 'new' territory. Thus in theory the statistical observation is simple. Each element in the region will be defined firstly in terms of the region's *per capita* immigration, and secondly, in terms of an increase in its *per capita* income, as a measure of marginal productivity. In the new territory the region must have a *per capita* immigration and an increase in the *per capita* income higher than the national average. These conditions will not be possible without a change in the economic structure, the appearance of industrial development poles and

[8] *Economic Development* (Constable 1959, p. 190).

the formation of nodal (polarized) regions. We have to turn to another technique.

Boundaries of Polarized Regions

¶The defining of polarized regions is most important for economic development. In new and growing countries, such as Latin America, the appearance, development, and integration of polarized regions is synonymous with the progress of industrialization and market economy. In older countries the identification of polarized regions stresses the location of the network of maximum economic interconnections and constitutes the best frame for the determination of efficient programming.

Even in older countries, the extent of these zones is not immutable, and their movement can be one of the objectives of economic policy. For this reason and others, two methods have to be discussed: (*a*) graph analysis, most practical for the descriptive determination of borders, and (*b*) gravitational analysis, more helpful to predict the movement of limits between two polarized regions.

(a) Graph Analysis

¶In a former paragraph we have used graph analysis to define a hierarchy. In studying the boundaries of regional influence of towns, the same technique provides us with a convenient tool.

The simplest approximation to inter-urban flows is given by road traffic on national highways. The necessary figures are available in almost every country. This traffic is mostly concerned with regional business interconnections.

A better test is given by the *network of inter-urban phone-calls*. Urban attraction is closely linked with information communication–with contacts existing between the different populations agglomerated in towns.

Every economic, social, and cultural activity is disseminated by mail and telephone calls. Although automatic exchanges make the problem of computation more difficult, it has been possible to obtain, in France, a good analysis of communications for 1953. It permits us to draw, for example, the boundaries of the information region around the regional metropolis of Lyon. The table gives us total telephonic communications; we possess only the two largest coefficients in a parametric matrix appearing as follows. It is sufficient to establish a loose binary graph.

centre	largest attraction	secondary attraction	
1 Bourg (Ain)	Lyon (Rhône) 47%	Macon (Saône et Loire) 43%	TABLE 5 Telephone con-
2 Privas (Ardèche)	Valence (Drome) 49%	Lyon (Rhône) 17%	nections in Alpes Region
3 Valence (Drome)	Lyon (Rhône) 22%	Privas (Ardèche) 25%	(Lyon) 1953
4 Grenoble (Isère)	Lyon (Rhône) 32%	{ Paris 19% Chambéry (Savoie) 14%	
5 Lons-le-Saulnier (Jura)	Lyon (Rhône) 21%	Macon (Saône et Loire) 16%	
6 St-Etienne (Loire)	Lyon (Rhône) 63%		
7 Le Puy (Haute Loire)	St-Etienne (Loire) 27%	Lyon (Rhône) 16%	
8 [Lyon] (Rhône)	Paris 16%	{ Grenoble (Isère) 18% St-Etienne (Loire) 16%	
9 Macon (Saône et Loire)	Lyon (Rhône) 43%	Bourg (Ain) 17%	
10 Chambéry (Savoie)	Grenoble (Isère) 32%	Lyon (Rhône) 21%	
11 Annecy (Haute Savoie)	Chambéry (Savoie) 35%	Lyon (Rhône) 19%	

	1	2	3	4	5	6	7	8	9	10	11	Population		
1								47	(43)			26,699 A.	(1)	Bourg
2			(49)					17				< 20,000	(2)	Privas
3		25						22				51,784 A.	(3)	Valence
4								32		14		147,358 A.	(4)	*Grenoble*
5								21	16			< 20,000	(5)	Lons-le Saulnier
6								63				184,619 A.	(6)	St-Etienne
7						27		16				< 20,000	(7)	Le Puy
8				18		16						649,507 A.	(8)	[Lyon]
9	17							43				25,835 A.	(9)	Mâcon
10				32				21				35,102 A.	(10)	*Chambéry*
11								19		35		38,414 A.	(11)	Annecy

TABLE 6   Structural polarized matrix of Rhône-Alpes Region (telephone calls and Answers)

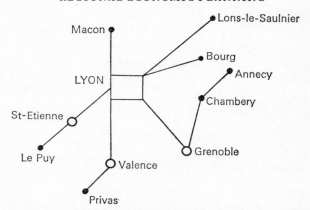

Graph of telephone
relations in Rhône-
Alpes Region, 1963

If Lyon has its heaviest traffic with Isère (Grenoble), it is because a large part of the conurbation is in this department. If we had the inputs (answers) separately from the outputs (calls), we would have to consider two different matricial classifications and borders. Our present matrix could be thought of as a synthesis of inputs and outputs. The same type of mapping would serve to discover the boundaries of influence of the different regional metropolises in Great Britain.

This is a purely *descriptive* and static technique. It does not give implicitly any explanation of the extent of polarization. For this very reason it cannot provide a forecast for any movement of the boundaries. This can only be done through a model explaining (or compatible with) the delimitation of the observed borders.

A first, and usual, model is the input-output *Isard Leontief* technical matrix. If we consider three regions (A, B, C), and in each of them three sectors (1, 2, 3) say *agriculture, industry, trade*, we obtain the inter-regional matrix on facing page.

This matrix, for basic input, has expenditure and import coefficients. The drawing of boundaries is aprioristic. Our aim is to discover the limitations within which the flows directly and indirectly within each region are minimized. This is on the three diagonal sub-matrices. The calculation should be made on the inversed $(1 - A)^{-1}$ matrix. Any change in structure will modify the design of boundaries.

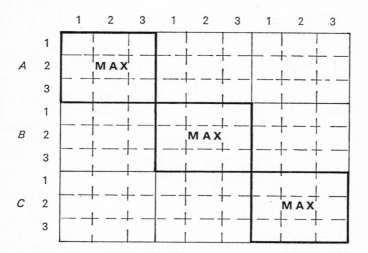

TABLE 7

Even this ponderous mathematical analysis is indeed much too simple, as we will point out in the next chapter dealing with instruments of regional policy. The proper approach is that of the propulsive industry in the propulsive region. Happily, we possess, as a first approximation, a global and more classical approach, known as *Reilly's law*.

¶A fruitful research method to explain the movement of the boundaries of polarized regions is the gravitational analysis expressed by Reilly's law. The universal gravitation law states that two bodies attract each other in proportion to their masses and inversely to the square of their distance $\left(F = \dfrac{M_1 M_2}{d^2} \right)$. In the case studied by Reilly a town appears as a gravitational pole around which smaller towns gravitate with their own satellites. Thus in the general formula above, M_1 and M_2 can be translated as the population of two towns and d the distance between them.

(b) Gravitation Analysis and Boundary Movement

If this law is substantiated, it would allow us to draw the boundaries of the polarized (attraction) zones of each town, given a *static* population. There would be no necessity for direct observation, measurement and graph analysis. Furthermore, the diversified growth rates of the *dynamic* populations in the different towns would enable us to predict and explain the movements of the boundaries of the polarized regions. But, although Reilly's law is close enough to observable reality, the position is indeed more complex, and we will have to qualify our former static and dynamic statements.

Reilly's law is the fruit of analogical reasoning, a most fertile research path. It is not, in fact, a gravitation law, but simply an information model relating the population of two towns in conjunction with the relative braking effect of distance. Indeed, the number of possible connections or business contacts between two populations M_1 and M_2 is $M_1 \times M_2$. The effect of distance d may be expressed as $\left(\dfrac{1}{d}\right)^\alpha$. This exponent should be, and is, different for each type of transaction: movement of different goods, telephone calls and movement of buyers towards markets and shopping centres, as in the original law of Reilly. A more general formula is thus:

$$F = k\frac{M_1 M_2}{d^\alpha}\ .$$

Exponent α is merely a distance elasticity of demand. Constant k depends on the units of measure. This law has been verified in France by means of a national survey conducted by Professor Piatier which involved the movements of fourteen different types of goods and services bought in every French town of under 2,000 inhabitants. Two methods are available to determine the distance elasticity coefficient of Reilly's law. The first is *cartographic*; though simple, this leaves out a great deal of the available information: it is the boundary method used by Delbes and the research group of Lyon.[9] It is nevertheless most helpful for a good approximation when the available funds are limited. The survey of buying centres gives us the boundary villages for which the attraction forces are equal. This equality of attraction of town A and B on the smaller centre C may be written:

[9] *Dans L'Espace Operationnel Macro-économique*, Cahiers de l'ISEA, Serie L No. 6; and L. Giraud: *L'Attraction Commerciale et La Loi de Reilly dans Croissance Economique et Poles de Rayonnement du Departement du Rhône*, Cahiers de l'ISEA, Serie L No. 7.

$$\frac{F_A}{F_B} = \frac{k\,M_A M_C}{k\,M_B M_C}\,\frac{(d_B)^\alpha}{(d_A)^\alpha} = 1$$

hence $\quad \dfrac{M_A}{(d_A{}^\alpha)} = \dfrac{M_B}{(d_B)^\alpha}\quad$ or $\quad \log\dfrac{M_A}{M_B} = \alpha \log\dfrac{d_A}{d_B}$

This is a simple logarithmic regression formula with $\log\dfrac{M_A}{M_B}$ and

$\log\dfrac{d_A}{d_B}$ on the axis. A point is determined for each boundary village. In the Rhône *departement* there were thirty-nine cases and points. These points were approximately close to a regression line. Reilly's law was verified and the slope of the line gave us a good estimation of the exponent. As far as general attraction was concerned the correlation coefficient was 0·95 and the exponent 2·7. Dairy products have a larger distance elasticity coefficient.

However, as Michel Robine[10] most accurately pointed out, such a method supposes that coefficient k does not differ from town to town. A better method is to use all possible observations for a single town A. The attraction of A, on a small village, may be written:

$$F_A = k_A \frac{M_A M_C}{(d_A)^\alpha} = k_A M_A M_C (d_A)^{-\alpha}$$

hence $\quad \log F_A = \log M_A + \log M_C + \log k_A - \alpha \log d_A.$

If we take all villages attracted by A and put, on a logarithmic graph, the distance d_A of the village to the town A on the abscissa and the ratio of the buying in A to the product of the populations of A and C on the ordinate axis, we obtain a descending line whose slope is the exponent of Reilly's law. The important point is that $\log k_A$ is the ordinate of the line at the origin and that k_A defines simultaneously the units chosen and the structure of town A. This type of study should best be made for every homogeneous group of products in order to ascertain a stability of behaviour as well as a necessary differentiation. Every homogeneous group of products has its own distance elasticity of demand.

[10] M. Robine: *Note sur l'Estimation Statistique des Paramètres de la Loi de Reilly* (Institut d'Administration des Entreprises, Bordeaux, 1964).

Anyhow, keeping in mind the preceding remark, Reilly's law is now verified in two ways. First, it has, in France, a total and synthetic application in the study of the zone of influence of large diversified towns of comparable structure (over 250,000 people). Secondly, in practice, the regression coefficient indicates that a distance elasticity of two is verified throughout the influence zone and not on the boundaries only.[11] Nevertheless, the regression coefficient is less significant for towns with populations between 100,000 and 250,000. The reason for this is that functional differences are much greater between the smaller towns than between the larger ones.

(c) *Dynamic aspects of boundary movement*

¶The above analysis leads directly to the *dynamic aspects of boundary movements*. These are explained by differences in the rates of growth between towns possessing the same type of structure, as well as by the evolution of urban structure within towns.

There are three points which have a direct practical application in this context. The *first* relates to a reduction in tariff consequent on the creation of a common market. This will require a well planned urbanization policy, in order to maintain the economic boundary on its previous political location, once the common market has been established. We have already seen an instance of this problem in Latin America, between Brazil and Uruguay. The *second* point is that the economic and sociological structure of a town is as important as its population size. For example, an important agricultural centre has not the same distance elasticity as an industrial city; nor will the regression line cut the ordinates at the same height. Thus a change in the production aspects of a town will bring a far greater boundary movement than could be explained by its population growth. The *third* point is concerned with the creation or the improvement of a transport route between two cities. The role, or rather the influence, which the route will offer one of the two cities is a power function of the distance, and the distance should be measured in terms of travel time taken.

[11] Jean Hautreux: *Les Principales Villes Attractives et leur Ressort d'Influence.*

The Reilly technique has been used by Leontief in a linearized version, and in connection with an input-output matrix to determine inter-regional flows. Therefore, it might be also used to trace the boundaries of the different regions. The boundaries in this case would be those giving values closest to reality in the result of the model. The method suffers from two grave dangers. First, these external exchange boundaries would rely on the validity of the model, and this has not yet been ascertained. Secondly, the external flows in a region, those studied by Leontief, are less stable than the internal flows. Consequently, the regional boundaries would be liable to shift more frequently. Therefore, we propose to adopt the former polarized regional concept; that of the internal and hierarchic network of maximum economic interconnection, which constitutes the best frame for the design of an efficient programme in a region. The value of our choice can be assessed, if we remind ourselves, once more, of the fact that economic boundaries are less intangible than political boundaries and that economic integration is easier to build than political integration.

Regional Economic Programmes

¶ The economic programme of a region, like that of a company, will depend on three sets of factors: (i) The objectives; (ii) the means available; and (iii) the economic structure. By structure is meant the stable mechanics of production, consumption, and trade prevailing in the region, just as in the firm.

However, the economic tools used in the analysis are different in the case of the firm and the region. The former is strictly private, whereas the latter is both public and private. And though the tools employed in the regional as well as in the company's programme will depend on the objectives, the region has a greater number of simultaneous relations than the firm. Thus there will not be, in the regional case, a direct deployment from means to ends. The different policies, e.g. wage policy, transport policy, or credit policy, will have a number of *indirect* consequences to be accounted for.

The other basic difference between the plan of a region and that of a firm is the *time horizon*. The optimum size of the programming region will vary with the length of the programme. Current management problems will be solved in the existing framework of a *departement*. Medium-term development problems (four or five years) will require the larger and more complex frame of a *programming region* to make feasible the co-ordination of investment decisions (as is the case today in

France, following decrees of June 2, 1960, and March 1964).

The long-term development evolution (fifteen to twenty years) necessitates an even larger *development region* to achieve the necessary co-ordination of basic investment. For this purpose, France, and Italy, have been divided into much larger development regions. In this chapter we are only concerned with the definition and implementation of the medium-term regional programmes, and, in particular, with the following topics: regionalizing a national plan; decentralization of regional planning; co-ordination between regional and national plans.

REGIONALIZING A NATIONAL PLAN

¶In Great Britain, as elsewhere in Western Europe, the first phase of regional economic action has been conceived at the national level. For example, in the United Kingdom, this action has been directed by the Board of Trade, and the *Distribution of Industry Act* dates from 1945. The *Local Employment Act* of 1960 has mainly been a reorganization of the abundant legislation on the newly named 'development districts'. The French legislation is very similar, although since 1964 it is better co-ordinated with the four-year plan which it is regionalizing. In Great Britain there is as yet no linkage between the Local Employment Act of 1960 and the work of the National Economic Development Council, created in 1961.

Thus, regions appeared at first, in every country, as local spots of unemployment within the national economic space. Regional life was not conceived as a polarized integrated whole, but as a homogeneous discontinuous space characterized by a high unemployment index – a 'depressed area'. The same state of mind prevailed as far as industrial location was concerned. No effort was made at the start to rebuild a regional economy. Plants were directed, in an arbitrary way, where work was most wanted. No effort was made to encourage regional firms as such. And most of the newly transplanted firms were not profoundly interested in the regional economy. Rolls Royce, ICI, or Unilever were of course associated with local employment and prices but their market and capital were dispersed throughout the country. Only after a long training and a large dose of information have the essentials and imperatives of regional polarized growth been clarified in Great Britain, as well as in France, through overall regional reports, programmes and plans.[1]

Economic regionalism was at first national in character. The point of this lies in the fact that the nation can assist the region, by embarking upon a complementary policy for spontaneous development as well as on a rational policy intended to stimulate new economic activities.

(a) Policy for spontaneous development

¶ The first type of policy is a liberal one, although the means to be used for its implementation depend on public decision. A national development plan will outline, for a given period of time, the targets to be achieved – let us say, the percentage growth of employment and the amount of necessary investment to be undertaken. It is therefore imperative to know the exact percentage growth pattern assigned to each region, in order that development can be stimulated through labour mobility, new trade channels, or the basic public investment needed for the attraction and location of new firms and the man-power requirements in the region.

To be realistic, it is necessary to plan the growth of industrial development poles and the movement of the rural labour force. In other words, public investment must be allocated within and between regions, having regard to some statistical indicators. At this stage, the idea of a region could even be abandoned since we assume that the distribution of investment is primarily between towns and counties. Nevertheless, a region remains a useful concept because it high-lights economic interactivity and contributes towards a well-knit coherent unit which is in no way spontaneous; as the Fourth French Plan has shown.

Generally speaking, basic public investment is understood to mean the infra-structure. It includes road and railway systems; water and energy supplies; education, housing schemes and expenditure on social and cultural environment in an industrial zone. The difficulty with public investment arises in the planning stage and particularly when a test for an accurate allocation

[1] e.g. Report on the Scottish Economy; Scottish Council (Development and Industry) under the Chairmanship of J. N. Toothill—(1962) Central Scotland: A Programme for Development and Growth. Cmd. 2188, November 1963. Plan for Scotland, 1966.

procedure is to be applied between the regions. A detailed analysis of the French procedure will be given in Chapter 6.

On the other hand, public action in a region aims at maintaining and encouraging, through financial provisions, *private* investment, without distorting free competition. For example, in France, the local firms in a region have access to, and can benefit from, the existing amount of savings, via the *Sociétés de Dévelopement régionales* which were set up by decree in 1955. These work hand in hand with the investment banks, and their task is to finance small and medium size firms by bond issues; however, the volume of business transacted is still small.

¶ The second type of policy (rational incitation policy), becomes necessary because industries tend not to operate in localities most favourable to national economic growth and development. This is the result of a number of external economic factors, and other collective costs. Firms tend to be located according to their own profit-and-cost criterion; most often in the large agglomerations. But collective costs are often greater in towns over and above a given size; labour mobility is a source of heavy expenditure and an excessive concentration blots out of existence all possibilities for innovation in the remaining smaller centres. For these reasons, as well as the difficulty in estimating direct and indirect social costs, a regional incitation policy seems fully justifiable. This policy aims at slowing down the rate of labour migration from the underprivileged regions and at the same time prescribing remedies for structural unemployment in regions traditionally well-equipped to tackle the problem but in which technical progress has been retarded. This is the point which Alain Prate stressed when he wrote: 'In the European Community, coal mining, a few years ago, accounted for eighty per cent of the total energy consumption, now it accounts for about fifty per cent and will amount to a third only around 1970'.[2]

(b) Rational incitation policy

In any event, external economic action can play a constructive role both at the national and regional level, provided that diversified industrial centres are created. These centres are called *dev-*

[2] *Marché Commun et Politique Régionale* (Revue d'Economie Politique, Jan./Feb., 1964).

D

elopment poles. This is a relatively new concept, and the technique underlying it is being constantly tested and improved. In Germany this is done in connection with the central industrial areas of the country; in the Netherlands in relation to development centres; in Great Britain with the creation of new towns; in Italy through the development of nodes and zones; and in France with the new 'metropolises', and 'poster' technique.[3] The means of such policies, conceived and promoted at the national level, are twofold: direct public action in providing the infrastructure, and indirect private investment. The relative importance of the first varies with the objectives to be achieved; whether, for instance, one seeks the development of small rural zones near industrial centres or whether one seeks to bring to life large peripheral underdeveloped regions where no modern industrial centre is available, e.g. the Mezzogiorno. For example, the public investment cost of the Taranto-Bari axis cannot be of the order of that of the Vogelsberg.

When the necessary infrastructure has been provided, the indirect impact which private investment can have on the plan becomes important. These investments can be made effective by loans, grants, and tax exemptions which the government may introduce. Unfortunately, this aid to industry is regarded as marginal. For example, in France between 1950 and 1961 only 14 per cent of all decentralization decisions took advantage of the special machinery and plant subsidy offered; simply because the administrative procedure was too complex. It has been substituted by a new, uniform and *quasi-contractual* system in April 1964, as explained in Chapter 6.

Such measures as these, planned and implemented by the central government, should logically constitute a regionalization of the national development programme, but can equally well be regarded as parallel to, and in co-ordination with it. This second possibility is common to countries without a national plan but with state aid to regions, whereas the first prevails in a country like France with indicative planning and an emphasis on co-

[3] See Chapter 6. In the West of France, we count eight poles: Brest Lorient, Nantes, La Rochelle, Cherbourg, Bordeaux, Toulouse, and Limoges.

ordination. However, this must not be confused with decentralized regional programming, described below.

DECENTRALIZED REGIONAL PLANNING

¶Today, regional planning through local authorities stems either from a federal, decentralized concept of the state; or from some type of administrative deconcentration and adaptation of region size to modern economics.

The minimum economic size of a regional programme can be conceived in terms of such small European nations as Switzerland and Denmark, similar to the Rhône-Alpes and North Region of France, with a population not exceeding five million and with a national income around two billion pounds sterling (six billion dollars). Scotland also, with a population of 5·2 million and a *per capita* income of £400 ($1,100) per annum, possesses the required size for self-economic management. Belgium and the Netherlands should be broken down into two regions. However, if autonomous development programmes were to be formulated for all the above-mentioned areas, it would be imperative for the central government of the country to be in direct charge, and responsible for the co-ordination of investment between the regions.

¶Autonomous regional programmes must be based on clear choice between objectives, and greatly depend on the available means provided by a decentralized or delegated economic decision. Thus the programme is shaped according to consultations and representations which the different organized bodies of the regions constitute.

(a) Autonomous programmes

In France, until 1965, there was no single comprehensive regional programme, although twenty-one regional memoranda, similar to the programme for development and growth in Central Scotland, had been submitted to the government. Their main objective was to inform and prepare public opinion for the final approach to a precise indicative planning. Also, there was the intention to establish the minimum essential favourable pre-conditions between the business world, trade unions, and the administration. The administrative reform of March 1964 has not radically changed the position. French

Regional Planning today is yet not very different from the first, national, stage, as propounded in the Monnet Plan. However, the reform created a *Préfet de Région* with certain economic and financial powers; and a consultative economic assembly, the *Commission de dévelopement economique*, which provides advice on public investment on a yearly basis. The regional plan, which is drawn up by civil servants, at the Regional Administrative Conference, and by the planners specially delegated[4] to the regions for a certain period of time, by the Minister of the Interior (Home Secretary), is based on public investment and on a few expanding regional industries, such as the chemical industry.

Important details of the plan will be left with the economic experts, who, together with the universities and the regional governmental statistical departments, can provide invaluable assistance, particularly when they are in close contact with the *Comités d'Aménagement*.

Discovering the Variables underlying growth

¶ Until now, regional research has been devoted to short-term projects, and on longer term population and labour-force studies. However, it is essential to recognize that this is not sufficient and that there cannot be a balanced regional growth without some knowledge of the basic economic structure of the regions and of the key variables underlying them – such as income, consumption, production, and investment.

The problems and difficulties involved in estimating these variables are formidable. A straightforward calculation of *public investment* in a region is faced directly with the problem of co-ordinating different administrative bodies (units) in their evaluations. In France, this has been partly overcome by the *Tranches Opératoires* procedure which enables the *Préfet de Région* to obtain directly, from the appropriate authorities, estimates of the volume of *public investment* for the whole of the plan as well as the proportion to be allocated in the following year.

However, this method does not coincide with the technique widely used for *private* collective investment planning.

The emphasis here is on capital coefficients obtained from an

4 They are preferably chosen in the region itself.

industrial census and taking the form of a number of ratios which indicate the stock of capital requirements for a given level of production and employment. Several difficulties arise, from the regional point of view.

The objective is to discover the value and productivity of investment, in other words the ratio of investment to added value and its correlatives: the ratios of investment to total sales, and of investment to employment. Mean coefficients are of little value, marginal coefficients are more significant.

The first difficulty is to secure the breakdown of investment by localized plants instead of total figures by companies. In France, these figures are, however, obtainable through the 1962 industrial census. But a single figure is insufficient to correlate investment and production, owing to the different lags existing between investment and production in each industry.

Thus the second difficulty is to dispose of accurate yearly information concerning total sales. But this can be computed through the employment figures available.

As far as investment figures are concerned, production lags have to be obtained, through direct enquiry. This being done, a correlation can be computed between investment and the growth rate of total sales of the economic sector (see diagram). If productive investment is computed separately, the intersection of the regression line with the gross investment axis will provide us with the value of amortization.

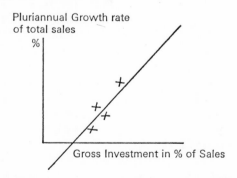

Pluriannual Growth rate of total sales %

Gross Investment in % of Sales

Another technique in shaping and controlling regional planning, despite its incompleteness, is *social accounting*. It is unfortunate that industry has not been made sufficiently aware of the usefulness of this technique. In France, even at the university level, only Nancy, Lille, Bordeaux, Caen, and Lyon have attempted to show its importance and to point out the difficulties in launching an input-output study.

However, social and inter-industry accounting requires that the size of the region must be large enough and, in consequence, sufficiently representative of all economic activity. Thus the Rhône-Alpes region in France, or Scotland, will qualify by definition for a study of this nature just as countries like Denmark or Belgium do. Moreover, for the study to be complete, it is necessary that the regional capital coefficients should provide the link between production, investment, and employment matrices.

The present technique of input-output analysis involves, at the regional level, two complementary approaches, which must be employed simultaneously. The first starts with the national accounts and regionalizes them. The second starts directly from local data on production and income. Of course, the first approach, starting from already elaborated figures, is the faster and, moreover, quite coherent with the national picture. The national account and input-output matrix is brought down to the regional level through an aggregation procedure which takes into consideration the special nature of local occupations. The discrepancies between national and regional aggregated coefficients are due to the difference in the relative importance of aggregated occupations on one hand and the differences in wage levels on the other. However, this approach assumes that there are no local peculiarities in technology, which is sometimes hardly true. This is why the second approach, starting directly from local data, is to be preferred. But it is much more difficult and far more costly. At the start, it will be to a large extent incomplete and will be useful mainly as a test and corrective to the first method.

The drawback of this double approach method is the great number of specialists required to gather the statistics and work out the complicated arithmetic and matrix computations it entails. Moreover, this way of using the facts for policy decision is not yet entirely understood at the regional level. Finally, the sociological unit of the region is not yet powerful enough to demand social accounts. There are a few exceptions, namely in federal states such as Germany, the United States and Canada, and (in the special case of Scotland), in Great Britain. In France, even typical regions, such as Brittany and Rhône-Alpes, are deeply divided between themselves.

¶A regional economic policy does not consist merely in drawing up and controlling the implementation of the programme in accordance with some central government method alone. Regional authorities require sufficient powers for political and economic autonomy. This may be restricted, in order to avoid the dangers embodied in the federal systems of Germany and Canada; but it does imply increasing financial autonomy, not only in the control of basic public investment loans but also in the fiscal policy, determined in relation to the local industrial activity. In France, the *Fonds National d'Aménagement du Territoire* makes loans to the local authorities engaged in matters of town planning and development. Also, the public savings banks (*Loi Minjoz*) may advance loans of up to 50 per cent of their deposits, to *departements*, municipalities, and chambers of commerce. However, any new industrial activity undertaken must satisfy the criterion of a current surplus in the revenue account; although in the first stages of industrialization the social structure may appear under strain, and increasing expenditures are required on behalf of the urban authority to maintain the momentum. Moreover, local taxes are not adjusted to the level of income, therefore a tax exemption on company income and expenditure could be a strong incentive to attract industry to the new areas. The complete absence of this measure partly explains why declining industrial towns are still the only ones pressing hard to introduce an industrial development policy.

The financial and fiscal autonomy handed over to local and regional authorities must not degenerate into 'imperfect competition' which could automatically produce unbalanced growth and consequently create a dichotomy between regional and

Regional powers

national interests. These fears necessitate a national co-ordination policy.

(b) National co-ordination of regional planning

¶A region or a federal state should not be regarded as an independent unit, but as part of a national whole, closely connected with other regions or states, and subordinate to national welfare. Of course, this subordination is subject to a regional constraint: the poorest region must not turn into a geographical proletariat; the growth of its regional *per capita* income must not be slower than the national mean. This entails help from the richest regions to the poorer ones. But does this policy conform to the attainment of optimum national welfare?

In fact, national co-ordination and arbitration derive from two different sources. The first source is inter-regional competition connected with some original form of unbalanced growth. The second source resides in the possible divergency of regional and national interests.

First, competition between regions may spring from unequal growth. Of course, it is not always harmful, particularly if it stimulates rather than retards the progress in the under-privileged regions. But the help given to the weakest regions may in its turn create further inequalities. It all depends on the regional complementarities and on the income demand elasticities for the goods and services produced locally. For example, the rate of growth in a rural region will induce a faster and greater rate of development in the neighbouring industrial region; because of interindustrial technical coefficients, as well as income elasticity for manufactured goods, which is greater than for food. Thus, if it is desirable to advance aid in the under-developed regions, it must be based on an industrialization programme requiring capital investment. 'Investment', writes Professor A. J. Youngson, 'may well give rise to a chain of further investments whereby the initial investment is sustained, elaborated and supplemented.'

This, together with the external economies created, is the most important element of what Professor F. Perroux has described as polarization investment. Thus regional depression and underdevelopment can be alleviated.

Regional inequality within a nation appears as a sequence of challenge and response, between which a centralized regulator plays the fundamental role as in any living organism. In any event, different regions tend to regard themselves as rivals, just as much as small nations within a common market. They are also rivals in their recourse to central government finance as a help to their local development.

In many ways, the problems arising from regional development are similar to those observed on a wider international scene. If capital, labour, and management migrations are easier between regions, this is only a reason for depressed or under-developed regions to fight this occurrence as hard as possible; indeed, for regions as well as for nations two main objectives exist: *welfare* and *influence* (polarization). These two objectives, more often than not, intersect but they do not coincide, thus making 'imperfect competition' between regions a very complex problem and difficult to analyse.

¶ The principal aims of maximum *welfare* are two; full employ- *Welfare*
ment and a rapid rate of growth in the *per capita* income. The attainment of these aims will be determined by the natural resources, the other factors of production possessed by the region, and the external relations with other regions. In effect, there are two types of economic instruments: domestic and foreign. The first is concerned with the regional wage, tax or investment policies. The second involves market research or patent policy. These influences are presently being studied at the European level. The EEC is in fact a large regional market in which the different member nations display the means suitable to their own end, which are far more numerous and varied in character than in the ordinary regional case.

Some of this economic policy can be managed with *supporting instruments*,[5] that is, instruments supporting each other from country to country, such as expansion or compression of government expenditures in a group of countries finding themselves in the same state of depression or in the same inflationary situation. Equally, there are *conflicting instruments* having

[5] The expression is that of J. Tinbergen, in *Centralisation and Decentralisation in Economic Policy* (North-Holland Publishing Co., Amsterdam, 1954).

divergent influences in different economies; such as the establishment of a common wheat price in agriculture systems at the community level or else the diversification of foreign exchange policies. Finally, some of this political influence will be 'neutral', because it will refer only to local conditions, goods, and markets or to the disposal of local income tax. Analysis on these lines, made as early as 1954 by J. Tinbergen, further stresses the point that regional decentralization can only be applied to narrow fields of economic policy, such as local taxation. In most other areas of economic policy it will have to be supplemented by administrative 'deconcentration', which is a mere delegation of decision to the regional representative of the central government.

Spheres of influence   ¶ Welfare is not the only objective of regional policy. The second objective, the increase in the sphere of *influence* or the exertion of some control over other regions, can primarily be measured in terms of the limits of the existing 'polarization' borders and their subsequent alteration or expansion. The regional metropolis, in order to extend its area of economic influence, will bring pressure to bear, by way of economic polarization, on other territories. This tacit warfare will eventually lead to the creation, enlargement, or annexation of 'satellite towns' by the metropolis. European urbanization and the formation of large and influential industrial cities renders this objective clearly intelligible. At the same time, the possibilities are created for genuine co-operation between regions, as is shown by the effort made in establishing economic borders between Northern France and Belgium.

Also, better awareness of the situation may accelerate the demand for speedier economic development in order to prevent gradual decline. One could argue that this is today the case with Scotland. But the opposite may equally well be the case, where there is a disassociation of political and economic borders, as, for instance, between Canada and the United States, or Federal Canada and the State of Quebec.

Another way to measure the area of influence belonging to a region is to estimate the domineering role which an industrial metropolis has on employment in other towns, through the

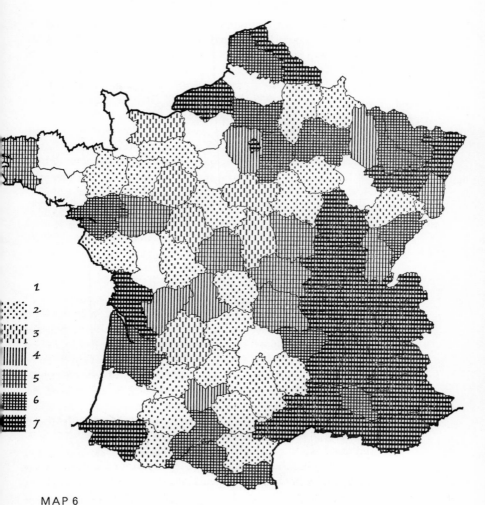

MAP 6

WAGE EARNERS CONTROLLED BY THE LYON REGION

The map shows the number of wage earners in each *departement*, in branches of business concerns whose head offices are situated in the built up area of Lyon. 1 : nil 2 : 1 to 24 3 : 25 to 49 4 : 50 to 99 5 : 100 to 199 6 : 200 to 399 7 : 400 and over (total 50,763, plus 26,076 in the built up area itself). Highest manpower : Rhône, 4192 ; Isère, 8629 ; Siene, 5620 ; Ardêche, 2973 ; Bouches du Rhône, 2858 ; Loire, 2739. Source : le Filâtre.

control, by parent companies, of their subsidiaries. This has been done already in the case of France by M. Le Filâtre, as shown in the table below:

TABLE 1
Employment
dominance and
dependancy
(France 1962)

	active population of the regional metropolis 1954	employment controlled by the metropolis 1962	employment controlled within the metropolis 1962
Lyon	320,293	50,763	61,437 of which Paris 53,158
Marseilles	283,284	15,452	28,578 of which Paris 23,222
Bordeaux	184,287	7,514	31,478 of which Paris 28,345
Nantes	103,821	10,161	26,014 of which Paris 23,382
St Etienne	84,081	18,598	9,319 of which Paris 6,806
Grenoble	65,496	5,651	11,184 of which Paris 8,237
Clermont-Ferrand	61,531	8,319	4,409 of which Paris 2,730

Source: Le Filâtre Commission Nationale d'Aménagement du Territoire, Groupe V.

The exceptional feature portrayed in this map (Map 6) is that the largest area of the connected *departements* is outside the programming region. This is also true in the case of Paris, Marseilles, and St Etienne; on the contrary, the two towns of Lille and Roubaix have their controlled employment essentially within the borders of their own *departement*, and the Pas de Calais.

This analysis illustrates even further the great importance and value of hierarchical decision diagrams and functional flow diagrams, when considering formal programming.

Bear in mind that the table and map illustrate the relationship which exists between the headquarters of the big commercial corporation and its subsidiaries, or between the large public company at home and its foreign branches abroad, and consider their importance to regional planning, taking into account their geographical distribution and pattern of behaviour.

A further useful distinction, in the fight for domination between regions, has been made by T. Haavelmo.[6] This finds

[6] *Economic Evolution* (North-Holland Publishing Co., 1954).

expression in the three strategies of 'grabbing', protection, and co-operation. Traditional competition theory studies productive activity. But other 'unproductive' activities exist, designed to interfere with the efforts of competing groups. In effect, there are two avenues to the acquisition of greater welfare, and therefore 'power'. The first is to produce more, and thus increase the sum of existing goods and services; the second is to 'snatch' part of another region's productive effort, in an otherwise unchanged total. The latter course implies a net gain with an 'unproductive' effort, but at the same time will automatically create a defensive action on behalf of the threatened regions. This commercial warfare between regions can be extremely harmful, particularly when the costs involved limit the possibility of more productive action. The best example is the demand for subsidies, between competing regions, from the central government.

The aid which the central government will be prepared to advance to the regional authorities, is to a large extent predetermined and limited by insufficient financial resources among competing ends, and by the scarcity of factors of production at any one time. For instance, it would be almost impossible, at present, for the French Government to undertake, at the same time, a Saône-Rhine canal and a Saône-Moselle canal, in order to join the North Sea with the Mediterranean.

A persistently wasteful effort to attain a lost cause will eventually slow down growth. Therefore, it must be replaced, under the central government's arbitration policy, by some measures of co-operation and compensation. The Columbia River Scheme, managed jointly by the United States and Canada, is an excel-, lent example of this point. Indeed, a river scheme may require, for optimum utilization of its energy,. the construction of reservoirs and the building of diversion dams in one country or region and a large river barrage with a power plant in another. The two states or regional authorities, acting independently, must not adopt a policy of leaving most of the costs in one and most of the benefits in the other. In fact, the cost-benefit evaluation will determine the basis of financial and energy transfer, thus maintaining the principle of equity in both states or regions and increasing total value added.

Co-operation may also be necessary in the case of industrial change. New industrial activity cannot be promoted and sustained simply by creating conditions of employment in towns and regions where unemployment already exists, without distributing this activity on some balanced social and economic scale. Today, the traditional coalmining districts are often faced with the difficult task of changing over to some other industry. This makes it essential to create identical policies between the established industrial zones near by and the emergent industrial pattern in the area. The developments in the St Etienne coalfield, other things being equal, should have been gravitating towards the Rhône Valley, where the transport facilities and power lines are to be found.

A national and regional campaign employing all the modern media of advertising should be launched, in order to stimulate sufficient interest whatever issues are involved.

Regional
Proletarianism
¶Economic change, of the type described above, may induce some form of regional proletarianism. However, this can be overcome, provided there is not an overall decline in the working population and that the regional income *per capita* increases at the same rate as that of national income. These assumptions do not restrict the mobility of the population, nor do they prevent emigration from the poorer to the richer regions. It is rather the number of available remunerative posts which can be provided by the poorer region, and the potential social progress offered by the rich region, which will determine the issue. The American experience, in the Far West, provides an interesting paradox. Between 1929 and 1949 this region attained an overall income increase of 227 per cent, but the *per capita* income increase was 10 per cent below the national average (admittedly today the gap is appreciably narrower). However, it still remains *the* immigration region of the United States, despite the fact that at the same time the north-east and southeast regions show the greatest relative increase in the *per capita* income (138 per cent). The explanation of the paradox is simple. The immigrants were the poorest among the people of the emigration regions and their income rose somewhat faster than average. Thus they improved their standard of living and con-

sequently attained a higher social status. Therefore, population movements and labour mobility within a region and between regions can be an asset to economic planning and development, and should be encouraged. Hospitality should be developed in depressed regions where the immigrant is always suspect. It is the unemployment situation and the regional depopulation which should be prevented and cured. One of the best solutions will appear to reside in a concerted economic policy.

The express aim of promoting the development of less productive regions at the same speed as that of more productive ones inevitably makes for wastage of scarce national resources and a slowing down of overall national growth. Some coordination between regional and national efforts must therefore be introduced. Furthermore, the regional administrative authority should not be an independent isolated source of claims and objectives but the model of economic efficiency. Even a federation, in order to function effectively, requires a powerful central government to establish and maintain the requisite social, political and economic code of behaviour.

In this context, and at a time when economic development and trade is discussed at an international level, it seems particularly odd to continue encouraging the negative aspects of regional viscosity. Nevertheless, the idea of planning in the region, both on theoretical and practical grounds, remains a useful one, in as much as it helps to create a larger local economic structure, especially where the original structure was too narrow for efficient operation on the modern industrial scale. In this, also, lies the explanation why diffused administrative decisions are preferable to decentralized political ones, especially when we begin with the urban planning level, and move up to the regional one. Naturally, the regional authority will strive to create conditions of full employment in the area, but this should not mean employment for *all* the local population. Moreover, if the policy adopted was one of isolation and staunch protection on behalf of each region, the outcome might sooner or later be uneconomic and against the public interest. At the same time, it might lead to some sort of antagonism, primarily based upon powerful policy instruments given to the region in eagerness to get the plan under way.

European
co-operation
¶ In France, since the introduction of the Fourth Plan, regional co-ordination has been implemented on the national level. In fact, the problem is better envisaged and solved within a European regional scale. The economic strength of Europe, and indeed its future political unity, may provide the solution to regional planning. The first signs of the disappearance of social tensions and prejudices in Europe are apparent today. These trends can be further encouraged by relaxing selfish regional attitudes and recognizing the valuable contribution which aliens can make to the prosperity of a region or a country. It may not therefore be a coincidence that in 1963 more than 700,000 foreign workers were employed in Germany; and that the Swiss economy draws as much as one third of its total labour force from other European countries. The state and federal economic policies, followed in America, provide another illustration of the thesis propounded by J. Tinbergen. A 'supporting instruments' policy, at the European level, will provide the desirable solution to regional planning – Keynesian full employment policy, with the emphasis on mutual agreement to promote co-operation between regions and national economic development.

INTER-REGIONAL CO-OPERATION

¶ To concert and consult together is perhaps the best way to promote co-operation between regional and national economic development. To achieve this objective, it is important that the administration should begin by acquiring a sound knowledge of investment forecasting and proceed to create and maintain an understanding between the businessmen and the trade unions, the other two responsible partners of the plan. However, in France and to a still greater extent in Britain, regional development plans appear to be handicapped by a 'time-lag' in this particular aspect of planning. This regional economic inertia is strongly connected with the methodological bias which survived in certain 'regional' professional circles, long after the Keynesian age ceased to be relevant. Economic thought, in the last ten years or more, has been post-Keynesian. Thus, we economists have the responsibility to proselytize an improved image of regional economic theory and the techniques which underlie it: namely polarization and propulsive industry analysis. Further, we should strive to achieve the required understanding through mutual agreement and technical advice. Several recent European examples illustrate the spirit of co-operation established through striving in concert, at the inter-regional level, both for medium-term growth problems and long-term development plans.

¶ Within the framework of medium-term growth two things stand out; first, the profitable ideas which emerge from inter-regional co-ordination; and, secondly, the practical difficulties of co-ordination, which can best be illustrated from the experience of administrative bodies in federal states. *(a) Medium-term growth*

Inter-regional co-operation is justified on the grounds that problems of general welfare are interconnected, binding contiguous regions together. Such problems include those of functioning and disequilibrium, and also of 'transmission' of disequilibria and growth. Therefore, co-ordination of trade and centralization of services between regions must be established. The diversity of regional economic structures is attributable more to complementary specialization in the production of goods sold in inter-regional and national markets than to differences in conditions of production. Thus regions are more often complementary to each other than in competition with each other. In the first case, regions provide reciprocal markets, whereas in the second they must learn to live in co-operation.

One of the fields of co-operation is the provision of precise and uniform description (through regional accounting and input-output tables) of inter-regional flows and influences. This involves studying the composition and volume of inter-regional trade flows. The intensity and variation of these flows is one of the most important but, unfortunately, least known sets of economic data. Various models must therefore be used for studying inter-regional trade, despite the fact that import and export flows are often not stable. Nevertheless, it is necessary to determine the process of instability in order to be able to construct a decentralized regional plan. The flows between one particular region and the others are confined mainly to the

E

transport of national goods. At a first approximation, they are sent by rail and water, whereas road transport is more concerned with movements of regional and local goods. Certain commodities constitute an exception (oil, wine, motor vehicles, electricity), and in such cases regionalization coefficients (nodal ties) must be directly obtained. However, for most national goods the coefficients may be computed from the railway matrix. Since 1958[7], the SNCF has published a square matrix for the various *departements* covering goods corresponding to twenty-five different tariffs, but which were established for commercial reasons and did not coincide with the economic classification of INSEE. A comparison of similar studies should be made at different points of time, based on a general inter-regional model, in order to assess the efficiency and variation of inter-regional trade flows.

The problems arising from the inter-regional 'transmission' of cyclical fluctuations and growth are equally important. Every regional development policy must take into account the consequences which its policy will have on the other regions. It may, therefore, be useful to have an industrial mixture between regions, such that cyclical trends will tend to cancel each other out. This problem of industrial composition between regions deserves separate attention, since the impact which the industries will have on regional fluctuations is very diverse. Some industries are *propulsive*. Propulsive industries are not those employing the largest labour force but those having the greatest direct or indirect influence on the welfare and activity of the region. They are highly concentrated and command at the same time a national market. Their activity influences regional income, which in turn will influence the trade and the services of the region, including the industries' own buying power. In brief, the activities of propulsive industries have a multiplying and polarizing effect which may be positive or negative. It is, therefore, important to know the relationship between the state of employment in the propulsive industries and the employment situation in other industries. A research project has been carried out for the Turin urban region by by Professor Lom-

[7] On a two year basis; since 1964, yearly.

bardini, based on the model of Professor Perroux,[8] to study this phenomenon. Some other research projects based on the present structure of active population in the industrial sectors and known as the 'basic employment' multiplier method appear somehow to be simpler. However, it is highly improbable that it would provide a good first approximation of complex dynamic relationships. Even in a more refined mathematical form it is incompatible with Leontief's input-output analysis, unless there should be a homothetic and utopian growth of sectors whose relative importance in the region is preserved. Nevertheless, *all* these studies are superficial because they tend to overlook regional interdependencies. Furthermore, we need to know the way in which fluctuations are transmitted and how the trade flows develop and decline. These can only be studied through the inter-regional flows *multiplier*, and not by the simple observation method of short-term fluctuations.

¶ It is within the framework of federal states that the difficulties of, and the solutions to, these rather complex problems can best be studied. First, there exists the accumulation of administrative experience by the federal government, in its dual role as an arbitrator as well as an assessor between the states; and, secondly, there is the availability of statistical information at the level which is required to carry out these studies: regional unemployment rate, growth rate, income *per capita*, and last but not least the interstate commercial flows. This is the case at present in Brazil and Canada. One day it may be the case in the European Economic Community. We shall take the Canadian past and present experience as an example, to illustrate the problems and solutions involved. The federal states of Canada (with the exception perhaps of Brazil) are among the few where a high degree of rivalry and diversity exists in their economic activity. This, however, has been transformed by policies of income equalization and economic aid to underdeveloped regions. Such policies have proved their worth and maintained the regional *status quo* without major disturbances to economic growth; at least if one is prepared to ignore the period between 1961 to 1964

Federal States and regional solutions

[8] *Modèle de Couplage d'une Région Polarisée avec une autre Région* College d'Economie Régionale, Liège, April 1960).

TABLE 2
Income *per capita*
in five Canadian
regions

when the economic influence of United States over Canada increased rapidly. The following table shows the evolution of income *per capita* in five large Canadian regions from 1926 to 1961.

Year	Canada	Atlantic Provinces	Quebec State	Ontario	Prairies	British Columbia
1926 ($)	—	277	360	486	457	515
1961 ($)	1,542	1066	1,332	1,829	1,435	1,795
income index (1961)	100	69·3	89·8	118·9	93·3	116·7
unemployment (1961) (rate %)	—	11·1	9·3	5·5	4·6	8·5

Source: Parenteau.

As we can see from the table, the Atlantic region is by far the poorest; it suffers from high unemployment and a low population growth. On the other hand, Quebec, although not as poor, has a high population growth which is responsible for the high unemployment rate. The provincial government's task, in each province, is to maintain all basic public services and to stimulate economic activity in general. To fulfil these objectives it must possess the financial resources necessary. Nevertheless, during the Second World War, the Federal Government took away from the provinces the right of direct taxation: income, corporate profits tax, and inheritance taxes. In exchange, and in order to compensate the provinces for the loss of revenue, the Federal Government advanced an equivalent high subsidy which was based on the indices of regional population and national income growth. Moreover, the creation of an income equalization system established a national financial norm for the allocation function of the federal state. Thus the same level of financial support *per capita* was discovered through these two combined types of subsidy. The level of the subsidy was determined by the average income *per capita* prevailing in the richest regions: Ontario and British Columbia. This system enabled the Federal Government to create large income transfers from the rich to the poor provinces. The following table will illustrate this point.

region	estimated direct taxation	perequation subsidy	total
Newfoundland	11·59	32·77	44·36
Quebec	29·36	15·00	44·36
Ontario	45·54	—	45·54
Br. Columbia	39·88	4·48	44·36

TABLE 3
Canadian subsidies
per capita
(1961-62)

Source: Parenteau

This 'equitable' system did not obtain overall approval, and was subsequently abandoned in 1962. In that year, the provincial governments regained their right to impose direct taxation at their own discretion. The income equalization subsidy was, however, maintained. Furthermore, the distribution of social benefits (payments) through the federal taxes, which by themselves create an income transfer, often as high as 12 per cent in the case of Quebec and as much as 17 per cent for the Atlantic Provinces, must be considered. Under the new regime, the Federal Government has also assumed greater financial responsibilities. It provides, together with the provincial governments, on a fifty-fifty basis, for public work projects, such as the Trans-Canadian Highway, and for the programme of hospital expansion. Federal norms can thus be maintained all over the territory.

Criticism of this kind of solution stresses the fact that the regular flow of subsidies, created within the system, do not succeed in providing the desired amount of polarization and induced investment. This, in a sense, comes closer to a system of social insurance than to the harmonized growth policy which was what it originally set out to achieve. A similar situation has long persisted in Italy, in the Mezzogiorno. It is this particular defect of the system which the French policy has tried to avoid by creating the development poles.

¶ The long-term regional programmes or plans, to quote Pierre Massé, are 'a geographic projection of a society's economic future'. They conceive economic space in a wider time horizon than the medium-term plan. At least a generation is required for changing the country's equilibrium position. Between now and

(b)Long-term regional growth

1985 the French national product will have doubled, the industrial scene will have been transformed with twice as many plants in operation as today, and half again as many households as at present. This prospective view of the economy can be a valuable instrument of policy-making, on which the long-term regional plan is based. We will study successively its geographic frame and its economic tools.

The plan is in itself primarily economic and rational. It can be regarded as a scheme of general orientation of economic affairs. It requires no sociological or administrative regional unity, as in the medium-term plan, because the co-ordination achieved in terms of the present social structure will be obsolete at the end of the twenty-year period with which we are concerned. Thus the socio-geographic frame of the administrative programming region is not relevant. To find another one, it is therefore imperative to explore two distinct types of regional questions: the first is of an homogeneous and the second of a polarized nature.

The first, in France, is manifested by the proletarian and de-population problem present in the west, which covers an area from Low Normandy to Bas-Rhône Languedoc and includes Auvergne. A simple projection of past population trends (1954-1962) has shown two separate effects. Although subject to index number problems, they are highly interesting. They try to distinguish two different types of process which engender the growth of total regional employment. Some regions expand because their industrial sectors have a swifter rate of growth than the national average. These leading regions in a country act as innovators and polarizers. They benefit from a 'differential' effect. This effect has shown that the west region of France is less dynamic in all its industrial sectors than the national average. Other regions expand because their economic structure causes them to participate more than others in the development of activities with the highest rate of growth. These regions, in which the proportion of expanding activity is particularly large, are intelligently specialized. To expand more quickly than regions less fortunately orientated, they do not need to have an above-average rate of growth per sector. They merely have to take advantage of the 'proportional' effect. This effect has also shown that, on the average, employment in France would increase by 16 per cent; 29 per cent in the Paris region, 18 per cent in the east and only 7 per cent in the west. The task ahead is enormous, if one considers the effort required to create adequate employment opportunities and hence to induce the right amount of investment in the area, which will assist to lift it onto the national average. However, it appears almost an impossible task, when taking 1962 employment figures. During that year, the west accounted for 37 per cent of the total employment, the east for 42 per cent and Paris (Seine, Seine et Oise, Seine et Marne) for 21 per cent.

The present regional frame can be changed and enlarged, through the concepts of polarization and growth poles, which in an industrialized country are the only means of sound programming. For example, the polarized region of Paris is larger than the three *departements* (Seine, Seine et Oise, Seine et Marne) which have been included in the 'Plan d'Aménagement et d'Organisation' would suggest. Moreover, the industrialized and growth zone of Paris, depicted by Le Filatre, is also larger. We can therefore infer that this region, which according to PADOG[9] estimates will be growing at a 29 per cent employment rate, will be growing even faster. We may, therefore, attempt to enlarge the frame of the region and instead of the three *departements* we will include seven of them: L'Oise with Senlis, Beauvaix, Clermont, Compiègne; L'Eure with Evreux; L'Eure et Loire with Chartres; and La Sarthe with Le Mans. These *departements* had a population of 10·5 million and accounted for 26 per cent of the country's employment. Under present estimates they would grow at least four times as fast as the west region and twice as fast as the national average employment rate.

This enlarged frame has a double advantage. It would not present, as an aid advanced to the western region, the rapid polarized growth of the Parisian PADOG, by way of the Loiret (Orleans) or the Sarthe (Le Mans). Also it would make explicitly

[9] Plan d'Aménagement et d'Organisation de la Région Parisienne, improved by the Schema directeur d'Aménagement et d'urbanisme (1965).

clear the need of diverting any spontaneous location away from this region towards other development poles which would be chosen as an equilibrium metropolis.[10]

The following table shows the importance and growth of three possible metropoles in the west compared with those in the enlarged Paris region.

TABLE 4
Equilibrium
metropolis in the
west and Paris
regions

	population, 1962	growth (1954-1962)
Toulouse	329,000	21%
Nantes	328,000	14%
Bordeaux	462,000	6%
Paris	7,400,000	15%
Le Mans	142,000	22%
Orleans	126,000	23%

It is interesting to notice that the most important western metropolis (Bordeaux) has grown at the slowest rate, whereas the satellites of Paris, Le Mans, and Orleans have shown the fastest rate of population growth.

This is one of the characteristics of geographical polarization and of the propulsive impact of the capital. Having analysed the geographic frame of long-term regional planning, we have now to study the problems of its own original economic tools; the classical production factors, labour, natural resources, and capital. As in the first case, this analysis will be done from two points of view: homogeneity and polarization. During the next twenty years, labour mobility will most probably reveal an interesting paradox of the French economy. The agricultural labour force will show a high degree of mobility with the inevitable decline of agriculture and the consequent growth of the economy as a whole. Moreover, this rural labour will eventually tend to migrate to Paris. On the other hand, the industrial labour force has traditionally a very low geographical mobility, concentrated within a close area, creating problems of industrial inertia. This kind of regional behaviour is contrary to the existing European trend of labour mobility. It may very well

[10] This has been done in another context, by the Delegation a l'Aménagement du Territoire (see Chap. VI) for governmental aid.

prove to be one of the great dangers of regional sclerosis in the future, hindering the supra-national development which to a great extent can be traced in rural origins.

Nevertheless, European evolution and economic progress will depend on the stable and regular supply of raw materials, the development of an adequate and efficient system of communications, the establishment of propulsive industries (which can benefit from the external economies provided by the large towns and cities of our civilization) and, last but not least, the liberalization of the investment flows together with the creation of new firms in order to palliate the deficiencies of local savings and the lack of entrepreneurial dynamism.

The flows of labour, capital, and organization have to be embodied within an urban frame which must be known beforehand. This explains the importance of the planning of the future metropolis and of its transportation network. It must be understood that for every town we have three different regions: the existing agglomeration; the urban and industrial region (of the PADOG type); the polarized region, including the satellite towns. This last region might even transform itself into some sort of 'nebuleuse' as the American urban formations studied by Gottman. In each of the regions a special transportation problem exists. All are parts of a large pantograph, and demand thorough programming techniques. We have described some of them in a little book called 'Les Programmes Economiques'.[11]

However, there is an aspect of agglomeration planning which is one of the directive notions of French urbanism and which has been crystallized by Paul Delouvrier.[12] A town which is no more than a juxtaposition of autonomous neighbourhoods would not be a city. The town is a centre of material and intellectual intercourse, it is a centre of freedom: freedom to choose a home, freedom to choose a job, to choose a school for each child, to choose friends and pleasures. The town is a gathering of high places – churches, theatres, and stadiums – unique for the whole

[11] J. R. Boudeville: Les Programmes Economiques (Que Sais-je, PUF 1963).
[12] P. Delouvrier: Avant Projet de Programme Duodecennal pour la Région de Paris (Imprimerie Municipale, 1963), and Schema directeur d'Aménagement et d'urbanisme de la région de Paris (1965).

agglomeration. This freedom and these symbols cannot survive without proper transportation planning.

We must not forget either that towns form a hierarchic polarized system through which economic growth will materialize. It must be remembered also that this urban frame will be set in a European environment and that the success of a European regional policy will depend as much on new and free inter-urban relations as on the growth climate and monetary stability.

Regional Operational Models

1: *Regionalization Models and National Planning*

¶The most useful concept in regional economics is that of the *programming region*. This concept involves the definition of practical objectives, and leads us to decide political measures and individual economic decisions alike, in order to attain given objectives in the most economical way.

Importance of objectives

A prerequisite, however, is the preparation of simple and pragmatic models free from excessive academic refinement, that will appeal to the private businessman and to the public administrator. Such models must clearly show the practical objectives to be reached, the social and economic structure to be respected, the financial and economic tools to be used. They must distinguish also between medium-term development (four to five years) and long-term planning of natural resources (twenty years). The models, too, must be based firmly on available statistical data and on existing economic tools, both public and private.

It is important to include *objectives* in models for collective action. Such objectives can conveniently be classified under two headings: (1) attainment of a higher regional welfare (income *per capita*, or terms of trade); (2) increment in size of regional influence, i.e. the extension of boundaries in the polarized region. The first set of objectives can be interpreted to mean a full-employment policy, and can be linked also with the relative trend of farm and raw material prices, or with the urgent need of the poorer regions to grow at a rate faster than the national average. The second set can be equated with a new regional network of towns and the selection of 'equilibrating' regional centres.

Several other important points deserve special attention: for example; how regional consumers and producers express their wishes; the conflicting and conciliatory character of the procedures in determining regional policies; and finally, how a regional programme is formed within the context of the national plan.

A principal characteristic of our approach must be insisted on. *Growth* may be pragmatically identified with a diverging set of rates; *development* requires the birth of new techniques and behaviours; *progress* is concerned with objectives. Progress is the shaping of an agreement concerning the aims and values underlying the economic development of the community. The so-called technical progress may be no progress whatsoever if it is not aiming at satisfying human wants.

This is why we will begin by examining regional *growth-models* within the framework of national planning, leaving for the next chapter the study of autonomous regional *development* and the choice of regional *objectives*.

Planning in most cases starts at national level and is progressively regionalized. In France, as well as in Sweden and the Netherlands, it has, from the beginning, been national in character. In Great Britain, the development of urban planning and of the New Towns' movement preceded the setting-up of the NEDC, and the National Plan, but it can be argued that these were really only forms of loosely co-ordinated help to depressed areas. Indeed, by present continental standards, the development of new towns cannot be regarded as representing integrated economic planning but merely technical programming mixed with some helpful sociological considerations. From the continental point of view, town, regional, and national planning should be parts of an integrated decision model, the aim of which is to maximize national welfare or to minimize national costs, including human and transport costs, within some constraints such as full employment and balance of payments equilibrium.

Moreover, it is statistically easier to work downwards from the nation as a whole than upwards from the region as an elementary unit. For example, *income* eludes precise computation within a cell so largely open to external flows and transfers. At first, *employment* seems to be the only reliable figure. Thus, the regional problem naturally appeared at first as a geographic projection of national programming. And regional operational models study employment before determining income and economic activity.

REGIONALIZING EMPLOYMENT MODELS

¶ In the long-term prospect (twenty years), both at regional and national levels we are confronted with similar difficulties, where *income* and *balance of payments* are concerned. Therefore, it would appear that employment is, in every case, the basic tool with which to identify desirable objectives and the means of attaining them. In this field, the United States has concentrated mainly on the study of historical evidence.[1] In France, the efforts have extended to the building of a decision model.[2]

Observational studies have shown that growth is spatially heterogeneous. This phenomenon is the cause of modifications to business and labour location. Description here is not enough. It is necessary to measure these modifications precisely, either for *projection* or for *prospective* planning. Bear in mind that projection is a prediction, and prospective is a policy. Three methods are commonly used: (i) the Dunn method, (ii) the Marczewsky, and (iii) the CNAT[3] method.

(a) Methods

Is the growth of a region the result of a favourable historical specialization, or of deliberate innovation and polarization? This is what the Dunn method[4] tries to elucidate. Indeed, it helps to distinguish between proportional effect (growth equal to national average) and differential effect (absolute deviation from national average).

(i) Dunn method

[1] Perloff, Dunn, Lampard, and Muth: *Region Resources and Economic Growth* (Johns Hopkins, 1960).
[2] C.N.A.T.: *Reports of Subcommission*, I. Mimeographed (Restricted).
[3] Commission Nationale d'Aménagement du Territoire.
[4] Cf. W. Isard: *Regional Programming* (O.E.E.C.); J. R. Boudeville: *A Survey of Recent Techniques for Regional Economic Analysis*.

TABLE 1 Measure of regional growth through proportional and differential effects (employment 1,000)

sectors	Rhône-Alpes Region absolute growth (1936-1962)				France growth rate (1936-1962)			
	(1)	(2)	(3)	total	(1)	(2)	(3)	total
(a) observed growth (statistical datas)	$_0e_1$	$_0e_2$	$_0e_2$	$_0E_R$	t_1	t_2	t_3	T
(b) Proportional growth (at national growth rates) t_1, t_2, t_3, T	$_pe_1$	$_pe_2$	$_pe_3$	pE_R				
(c) differential growth $c = a - b$	$_de_1$	$_de_2$	$_de_3$	dE_R				

Note: $\sum\limits_{1}^{3} {_0e} = {_0E_R}$ and $\sum\limits_{1}^{3} {_pe} + \sum\limits_{1}^{3} {_de} = {_0E_R} = {_pE_R} + {_dE_R}$

$\sum\limits_{1}^{3} {_pe} = {_pE_R} + \Pi$ and $\sum\limits_{1}^{3} {_de} = {_dE_R} + \delta$

hence $\Pi + \delta = 0$

In table 1 we have sketched the growth of a French region (Rhône-Alpes) and of the national economy, through three sectors, taking into account the active manpower. The first line (*a*) shows observed regional growth between 1936 and 1962. The second line (*b*) shows what the growth would have been on national standards (proportional effect).

It is important to note that the calculation, on sectoral and total figures, gives different answers. This is due to the structural differences existing in national and regional economies. Indeed, we find the same absolute values but with reverse sign at the proportional and differential levels. More important is the meaning attached to the absolute values of proportional and differential growth in each sector. The differential effect actually conceals the innovation and polarization mechanisms, whereas the proportional effect is supported by regional specialization and relative cost advantage. If differential effect is not a sufficient explanation of development, as we will see later on, it is nevertheless quite useful in distinguishing between regions which have merely grown through structural and natural resource advantage (Lorraine region) and those which have taken advantage of, or compensated for, this fact through differential dynamism. The following table illustrates this situation.

TABLE 2 Regions classified through proportional and differential effects

| | | proportional effect (p) | |
		favourable	unfavourable
differential effect (d)	favourable		
	$d>p$	N_1	N_5
	$d<p$	N_2	n_6
	$d<p$	N_3	n_7
	unfavourable		
	$d>p$	n_4	n_8

Note: N = number of regions growing faster than the national mean.
n = number of regions growing slower than the national mean.

(ii) Marczewsky's method

Table 3 can be attributed to Marczewsky's analysis[5] of the French national growth rate, which is somewhat different. The proportional or structural effect is taken into account through weighting. Thus Marczewsky considers the arithmetical average rate of growth as AR, the weighted rate as WR and their relation as $WR/AR = \rho$.

It goes without saying that the weighted rate takes into account the initial importance of the different sectors, whereas the arithmetical rate does not. The difference between the evolution of the two rates denotes a structural change. These changes may be favourable or unfavourable as shown in Table 3.

The conclusions which can be drawn from this table accord

[5] J. Marczewsky, in the Round Table I.A.E.S., (Constance, 1960): *Le Take-off vers un Croissance Soutenue.*

TABLE 3

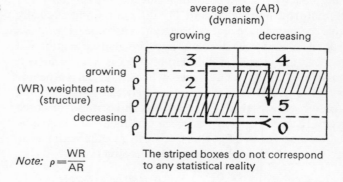

Note: $\rho = \dfrac{WR}{AR}$

The striped boxes do not correspond to any statistical reality

with the French regional growth problem. Box 0 represents the case where there is a slowing down of growth in spite of the creation of new industries (small weight). Box 1 shows a case of growth through the development of new industries and despite the decline of traditional ones (heavy weight). Box 2 denotes a growth which can be attributed more to the creation of new than to old industries, the latter being stimulated by the former. Box 3 is the situation where the first signs of the ageing regional structure appear; new industries grow less rapidly than old ones. Box 4 demonstrates some stability in the old industries and a decline in the new cases. Finally, Box 5 is the case of a joint decline.

This type of analysis, which can just as well be used for each nation as for each region, can adapt to fast structural change through chain indexes. Therefore, it can best describe countries where this has been important, namely, Great Britain and France.

(iii) CNAT *method* It is not sufficient, however, simply to describe past evolution and project it into the future. It is necessary to discover a 'future' different to the projected one. The objective has to be set, its consequences measured, and the ways and means which will achieve it checked with reference to a '*laissez-faire* growth'. In effect, this is the difference between forecast and *prospective long term programming*. This is the method which the Commission Nationale d'Aménagement du Territoire (CNAT) has been exploring. The planning objectives in France are set for 1985. The first step is to build an objective which will be different from a simple projection, in order to create a maximum of 'reasonable'[6] employment in the poorer region, i.e. the west of France. Under this assumption, France has been divided into three long-term regions: Paris,[7] East and West.

The comparison of spontaneous employment growth and prospective employment is set out in the table below:

	East	West	Paris Padog	Σ
projected spontaneous regional growth	+1·4	+0·3	+1·3	3·0
prospective growth	+1·2	+1·0	+0·8	3·0
shift	+0·2	−0·7	+0·5	0

TABLE 4
Projected and prospective employment, France 1962-1985 (million jobs)

Note: The computations have of course been made for each of 28 sectors of production. Figures are rounded and illustrative.

The total increase of employment is evaluated at three million jobs (twenty-one million, instead of eighteen if left unchanged), but the table envisages 700,000 jobs being created by 1985 in the West Region at the expense of the Paris urban zone (500,000) and the East region (200,000). What this means is that this labour force will remain in its home region rather than emigrating. In effect, this is the first tentative objective which has been set by *group one* of CNAT. How it will be realized is the responsibility and task of the other groups. The most important of these is the urban structure group. It is estimated that by 1985 the active rural manpower will be only 10 per cent of the total. Hence 90 per cent will be employed in towns, which shows the link between industrial location and urbanization. The task of the urban structure group is, therefore, to determine the shape and number of regional metropolises, especially for the underprivileged West. These will have to be associated with large development poles, which means weighting external

[6] By 'reasonable' is meant, as a first approximation, what is thought to be possible by a large sample of large and medium size firms.
[7] Taken here as Seine, Seine et Oise, Seine et Marne: PADOG urban zone, and not as the large polarized region of Paris.

F

economies and minimum transportation cost with migration costs and external diseconomies.

(b) *Regional employment multipliers*

¶Prospective employment in a region cannot limit itself to *projections* and the measure of differences between desired objectives and probable evolutions. With the French method of a reasonable employment goal in mind, to ask businessmen what is possible in terms of evolution, is to place before them an incomplete and insoluble problem. They cannot, from their own sector, grasp the whole problem of national and regional interdependencies and harmonized growth requirements. A special planning procedure known in France as 'concertation' is needed to attain harmonization. Indeed, with every production growth two phenomena arise. The first involves an additional distribution of income. These incomes are spent differently on each product or sector, resulting in an unequal growth among consumer industries. The second phenomenon is concerned with the intersectoral supply of the different industries (input-output table). Inter-industrial inputs will grow at different rates in order to satisfy the unequal rate of growth of the final demand.[8] Finally, harmonized growth is the set of diversified growth rates reconciling supply with demand in each sector, and therefore avoiding price distortions and other social strains. Consequently, it is not pragmatic but Utopian to ask the *entrepreneurs* to make individual long-range (1985) forecasts of their reasonable growth. Isolated market surveys, as well as possible increases in productive capacity, are not realistic at this level. The growth of the motor-car industry in the past twenty years provides us with a good illustration. Multiplier accelerator and polarization mechanisms come into action. Fortunately, the problem can be tackled through a rough estimate, based on the available regional employment data. Analysis akin to the Keynes multiplier can be applied globally to each town, if the proportions of active manpower working for the local and the external

[8] *Uniform growth*, as studied by Cassel, Samuelson, Solow, and Radner, appears as the long run equilibrium in a 'dynamised' Leontief model which assumes: constant consumption parameters, no substitution between labour and capital. In this model, deviation from uniformity is due to deviation of initial values of the variables from what would correspond to long-run equilibrium.

markets are known, and are supposed to remain constant. This approach is known as the *basic employment multiplier*.[9] It describes the impact which the export industries of a town have on total activity. Firstly we can write a definition equation:

(1) Total employment (E) = Local employment (L) + Export employment (X).

Further, if we consider the *a priori* hypothesis that local employment is a fixed proportion of total employment in each town,[10] it can be written as follows:

(2) $L = KE$, where K is a *constant*,

Hence

$E = KE + X$, and

(3) $E = (1 - K)^{-1}X$. This is nothing else but the multiplier concept as devised by Keynes or Leontief.

Nevertheless, it would be inconsistent to matricialize such an export multiplier and to combine it with the input multiplier of Leontief.[11] We shall illustrate this with a simple example. In every town, each sector has a *national*, a *regional*, and a *local* employment market. Sector one has a total employment E, which is composed by L (local employment) working for the local market, R (regional employment) working for the regional market, and N (national employment) working for the national market. We can represent this in a table of corresponding coefficients.

	local	regional	national	total
sector 1 (%)	l_1	r_1	n_1	1
sector 2 (%)	l_2	r_2	n_2	1
sector n (%)	l_n	r_n	n_n	1
total (%)	l	r	n	1

TABLE 5
Sectoral distribution of local, regional, and national employment

These coefficients are observed percentages and not statistical constants. In fact, they vary much more for each sector than for

[9] Cf. Lucienne Cahen and Claude Ponsard: *La Repartition Fonctionnelle de la Population* (Ministère de la Construction, Roneo 1963).

[10] This hypothesis has no sound statistical foundations.

[11] See, however, Lee Hansen and Charles Tiebout: *An Intersectoral Flow Analysis of the California Economy* (The Review of Economics and Statistics, November 1963).

all sectors taken together. Similarly, they vary more in a growing town than for the towns of same rank and size in the whole country.

In addition, if we were to work with the Leontief technique of *input* coefficients it would be impossible at the same time to work with this previous technique of constant sales or output coefficients. The mathematical proof is simple: an input coefficient has the form: $A_{ij} = \dfrac{X_{ij}}{X_j}$; which means unit consumption of product [i] by industry [j] divided by total production of industry [j]. An output coefficient has the form: $C_{ij} = \dfrac{X_{ij}}{X_i}$; which means total sale of product [i] to industry [j] divided by the total production of industry [i]. Therefore, $C_{ij} = A_{ij}\dfrac{X_j}{X_i}$.

If we return to the Leontief hypothesis and take A_{ij} to be a constant, C_{ij} cannot also be constant unless $\dfrac{X_j}{X_i} = K$, which means a Utopian homothetic growth. Thus the basic employment multiplier should be purely based on the Keynesian 'global' income analysis.

If R_1 stands for local income, R_2 for regional income, and R_3 for national income, we may write for each of our n sectors—

$$E_1 = a_{11}R_1 + a_{12}R_2 + a_{13}R_3 + b_1, \; i = (1, 2, 3, \ldots n).$$

$$E_n = a_{n1}R_1 + a_{n2}R_2 + a_{n3}R_3 + b_n$$

However, no complete statistical correlation has yet established the Keynesian regressions. Consequently, we are forced to conclude that for the time being the basic employment analysis is not an adequate tool to provide us with the answer, because in the short run the coefficients suffer from excessive instability, and in the long run the structure is liable to modifications. With this in mind, the French economists acted wisely in basing their estimates on the employment multiplier on a 'global' level, although the statistical investigations were carried out originally under different assumptions.[12] To arrive at a sectoral multiplier

[12] Cahen and Ponsard, op. cit.

it was found necessary to establish an input matrix for each of the eight regional metropolises of France, plus one for Paris. The cost of such studies is almost prohibitive, especially if the starting point is the investigation of private firms.

REGIONALIZING INCOME AND ACTIVITY

¶ Practical reasons justify our starting from national accounting and medium-term national planning, in order to approach successfully the problem of investment location and regional development proper. Here we shall consider three different models:

(a) Regionalization of investment in national planning;
(b) Regionalization of the national input-output matrix;
(c) The special case of the agricultural complex.

¶ The method of national planning has been examined in Chapter 3. Therefore, we need only stress how the allocation of investments within the different sectors of the economy is determined, in order to reach a national target, i.e. an annual rate of national growth within certain constraints; say, the balance of payments disequilibrium and the relative level of *per capita* agricultural income.

(a) Regionalization of investment in national planning

The total volume of national investment is predetermined for each sector. It thus becomes possible to rank individual projects inside each sector, through benefit-cost ratios, as advocated in the United Nations Manual on economic development projects.[13] These valuations and their impact (secondary effects) become more comparable. Also, the selection of one aim (income increase) and the consideration of one scarce factor only (capital invested) becomes more appropriate. By such means, the maximum increase in income will be obtained from the planned amount of investment. This is similar to the method used by private businesses, except that increases of income to be taken into account accrue to the nation as a whole instead of being received by private investors only. Further, the study of

[13] *United Nations Manual on Economic Development Projects*, New York, 1958.

individual projects makes it possible to take account of the time involved through production lags and distribution effects, as well as through technical progress and the evolution of marginal capital coefficients over time. Thus the original capital coefficients of the plan may be revised. Individual project studies enable us also to take account of technical indivisibilities and minimum scales of production. From the regional point of view, the important thing is that the choice of these individual projects dictates a specific location for a large number of them. This is the case with dams, roads, bridges, harbours, and firms concerned with the exploitation of natural resources. If the total of these amounts to 40 per cent of national investment, 60 per cent only is free for regionalization; that is, for allocation to one region rather than another, following predetermined criteria.

In a national space the decision model does not discriminate and imposes no constraints stemming from the regions. Regionalization implies that a new function must be included to permit an accurate division of the total population and to incorporate the contiguity constraint characterizing the concept of a region. This is the determining of the regional boundaries. Having successfully introduced this new element into our model, we proceed to interpret this geographical division in terms of economic objectives and constraints. Finally, we have to incorporate these regional subsets into the national set.

Clearly, there are three steps to be taken:

(a) the division of national space through a regionalization function (determination of boundaries);
(b) the accounting for the regional constraints;
(c) the checking in each region of the predetermined national location constraints.

First step *The first step* implies the choice of a regional criterion: homogeneity or polarization. In industrialized countries growth is polarized. Thus it seems that polarization would be the most appropriate criterion to choose for the majority of countries in the western world (underdeveloped regions of Latin American countries are an exception). We assume that two poles, $[i]$ and

[*j*], are predetermined. Thus the regionalization function of [*i*], if we call sTi the transaction of a satellite town [*s*] with pole [*i*], and sTj its transaction with pole [*j*], may be written as $sTi \geqslant sTj$. If this condition is satisfied, satellite [*s*] belongs to polarized region [*i*] which determines also the population in question.[14]

This regionalization function may be expressed in a graph. We have seen examples of this in Chapter 2, where every transaction matrix had its associated graph. If, on a total transaction matrix, or more often on a 'significant' one, we retain only the most important flow in each connection vector (subset), we are left with a binary graph determining a transitive ordering. This type of ordering coincides *in fact* with a geographical contiguity constraint. This constraint can be expressed by the expression $dis_i < dis_j$, where *d* means distance, and if s_i is a satellite of pole [*i*] and sj a satellite of pole [*j*] located on the same radius.

Let us assume that the division of the national space into polarized regions has been achieved, or at least, that an administrative division has been decided on. This division of space may be thought of as the establishment of programming regions. Within this frame of reference a national distribution of investment can be expressed in proportion to the importance of activity in the different sectors of each region (proportional effect). This enables us to compute (1) capital investment per head in each region, (2) average rate of growth in the *per capita* income, and (3) rural emigration, by the regression formula $Pr = aR + b$, where Pr is the rural population and R the regional income. The correlation coefficient between these two variables is known to be around 0·9.

The second step deals with regional constraints. Two of these *Second step* are very important. The first is the maintenance of a minimum population in depressed agricultural regions. This means that agricultural migration, as opposed to demographic increase, has to be absorbed by industrial and tertiary growth. This growth includes employment opportunities created directly and indirectly within the region. Thus some sort of employment multi-

[14] The relation defining the polarized region of (*i*) may be written: $Ri = \{sij \mid sTi \geqslant sTj\}$

plier has to be computed. The simplest form would be a regional basic employment multiplier, whereas the most refined one would be based on regional accounting and an input-output matrix.

The second constraint is the prevention of relative decline in the regional *per capita* income (this is a tough objective, since the poorest regions are most often those growing at the lowest rate). The problem would be easier to solve if a national constraint (of relative increase in rural *per capita* income) were imposed on the economy. But this is seldom the case.

Third step   *The third step* is concerned with regional allocation of investment. This arises because we are not certain whether a regional distribution of projects which is ideal from the community's point of view will coincide with a proportional regional distribution of investment. It is most likely that this will not occur; but to what extent?

As we have said, the location of a large part (40 per cent) of national investment is regionally predetermined by natural resources, existing urban markets, local wage levels, and demographic increase. What is left (60 per cent) is often called 'location free' investment and is the material for regional programming. This comprises the expanding light industries such as electronics, machine tools, tourism, and a small part of public works. If no room is left for them, a second-best national choice has to be made. In order to arrive at a precise solution we must, however, obtain a more refined set of data on regional connections (i.e. a regional inter-industry and social account) than is often the case. A study of this kind can be long and costly. Happily, a reasonable accurate approximation can be obtained for large interconnected regions (e.g. Rhône-Alpes) through a regionalization of national accounting.

(b) Regionaliza-   ¶Regional accounting can be achieved through two possible
tion of national   methods. The first is precise, but difficult to co-ordinate with
accounting   other regions and with the nation. It is an 'upward movement' starting from the accounts of regional firms and family expenditure budgets, and ending with the regional economy as a whole. The second method has the virtue of being more coherent but

can be said to be less precise. It is a 'downward movement', from the national level to the region. The aggregation and equivalent transformation techniques help to make it a ready-made and useful analytical tool. Technical progress and price disparities can be introduced for a number of sectors through this method.[14a]

In fact, inter-regional flows differ from national ones in three ways:

(i) technical coefficients are different;
(ii) regional prices are on different levels;
(iii) the larger part of trade is external.

It is worth while exploring these differences further. The special character of regional *technical coefficients* is due to two different causes. The first can be attributed to the special composition of the regional sectors. In a twenty-eight-branch matrix, the subset composition of each branch differs from region to region. The different weights of the sectors which we include will modify the aggregated technical coefficient. This is quite clear in the case of France, when, in each region, we reduce the number of sectors, for example from sixty-five to twenty-eight and then to eighteen. The second cause is due to particular regional techniques. Direct enquiry is needed. As a first approximation it can be postponed for most sectors.

As far as regional prices are concerned, the most important factor which accounts for the difference is the wage level. It has a cost impact on the matrix which can be taken care of by a similitude transformation. More generally the evolution of the price level can be equally integrated in the same manner.

Finally, the problem of external trade in a region is the most difficult one to cope with. It is nevertheless one of the most important. To compute the impact of regional or external changes in prices or activity it is necessary to know, for each sector, the proportions of domestic and import expenditures. The enterprises themselves are generally unable to give such precise information. They know their inputs; they do not know

[14a] Richard Stone: *A Computable Model of Economic Growth* (Chapman and Hall, Cambridge, July, 1962.)

where they come from. The only direct statistical source is therefore transportation. From this point of view, the French railway transport matrices for each of the eighty-nine *departements* and twenty-six categories of goods are most useful. Unhappily, this tariff classification is linked with railway transportation costs, not with the technical nature of the products. It is impossible to reconcile it even with the eighteen-sector matrix. The creation of an obligation on the railways to provide statistical data corresponding to this classification is of the highest importance if the western economies wish to have accurate regional planning. In France, the only sector in which an interregional input-output matrix is available is *energy*. It has been established by the CEREN[15] for Coal, Petrol, Fuel, Gas, and Electricity (eighteen branches), and is completed by a balance sheet. In other sectors indirect methods are used which are highly hypothetical. Before sketching them we will deal here with the first of our three problems; more especially with the *regional aggregation of the national matrix*.

Aggregation of national matrix

¶ To make this technical but basic problem as simple as possible, let us take an example. In 1959 the SEEF[16] constructed a sixty-five-sector output table. The national technical coefficients for that year were calculated, by dividing the differing consumption of each sector by the production of the same sector at market prices. This may be written as follows:

$$A = Z\hat{X}^{-1}$$

A is the technical matrix, Z the input-output table and $\hat{X}$ the diagonal matrix of the production vector. If instead of using national weights we use regional ones, this matrix may be aggregated into a twenty-eight-regional sector matrix, or even an eighteen-sector matrix. The weighting will be done not simply by employment figures alone, but by production values. Production values can easily be obtained provided we assume the same productivity per head at both regional and national level. Thus national production per worker in one sector is multiplied by regional employment in the same sector.

[15] Centre d'Etudes Régionales sur l'Economie de l'Energie.
[16] Service des Etudes Economiques et Financières du Ministère des Finances.

To avoid the long and rather difficult problem of weighting technical coefficients, we may calculate the regional input-output figures directly from the large (sixty-five) input-output table, and thus obtain by a simple summation an integrated regional eighteen-sector table. We then proceed to calculate the coefficients in the usual way. Any year-to-year variation can also be computed, together with employment, if this is necessary. Thus weighting modifications become automatic. In fact, the formulation of an aggregate based on a coefficient matrix has the advantage of showing the important role which the basic 'year weights' carry.

An aggregation of the following type:

$$A = \begin{bmatrix} a_{11} & a_{12} & a_{13} \\ a_{21} & a_{22} & a_{23} \\ a_{31} & a_{32} & a_{33} \end{bmatrix} \quad \text{with activities} \quad \begin{vmatrix} x_1 \\ x_2 \\ x_3 \end{vmatrix}$$

may be written as:

$$A^\star = \begin{bmatrix} \text{I} & \text{I} & \text{o} \\ \text{o} & \text{o} & \text{I} \end{bmatrix} A \begin{bmatrix} \beta & \text{o} \\ (\text{I}-\beta) & \text{o} \\ \text{o} & \text{I} \end{bmatrix}$$

where $\beta = \dfrac{x_1}{x_1 + x_2}$ and $(\text{I}-\beta) = \dfrac{x_2}{x_1 + x_2}$

The matrix $\begin{bmatrix} \beta & \text{o} \\ (\text{I}-\beta) & \text{o} \\ \text{o} & \text{I} \end{bmatrix}$ is thus the basic year weighting matrix and the transformation of A is an equivalent transformation.

The former procedure is important for the years preceding the regional results of the French industrial census of 1962. It is also useful to make a distinction in this given year between what we shall call the regional *technical* effect and the regional *specialization* effect.

Indeed the difference between an aggregated national input-output matrix and an aggregated regional matrix of the same order can stem from two sources: (1) the unequal relative importance of the aggregated subsectors; (2) their different technical characteristics. The interest of such a distinction is to evaluate the impact of a possible technical improvement in a given region. The specialization effect is given by the regionalization (weighted aggregation) of the national matrix. The technical effect is obtained by computing the difference between the direct regional matrix and the regionalized national matrix.

Of course, what will still be lacking after the exploitation of the 1962 industrial census will be the knowledge of the extent to which the regional activities make use of regional goods. To suppose that they give them priority, and consume external goods only if regional production is insufficient, is simply an heroic assumption. Cross haulage is obviously frequent from region to region and special models only can take them into account. The best known is the latest Leontief attraction model which we will describe later on.

Concentration ratios   ¶Less precise are the indirect methods which measure the regional 'opening' to national and international economic flows. They may be described as a first approximation, by concentration coefficients. It is important to stress that these coefficients enable us to decide whether a region imports or exports a given type of product. If a particular industry happens to be concentrated in one region, rather than spread all over the country, it is assumed that it has a 'location cost advantage'. Therefore it is inclined to sell its output on a nation-wide market. A simple form of concentration can be measured through the number of people employed in the industry. In France, three concentration ratios have been defined:

(1) *Departement* concentration—$S = \dfrac{e_{jd}}{E_d}$ where e_{jd} is *departemental* employment in sector j and E_d is total *departemental* employment;

(2) *Regional* concentration—$P = \dfrac{e_{jR}}{E_R}$; and

(3) *National* concentration—$V = \dfrac{e_{jn}}{E_n}$.

From these three ratios six different combinations emerge:

$S > P > V$ National industry dispersed in a region
$S > V > P$ National industry concentrated in a *departement*
$P > S > V$ National industry is less concentrated in a *departement* than in a region
$V > S > P$ Regional industry
$P > V > S$ *Departemental* industry prominent in the region
$V > P > S$ *Departemental* industry not prominent in the region.

This classification has been used in a linear transport model for the Rhône-Alpes region.[17] The exporting regions are, at a first approximation, those with a concentration coefficient P larger than the national average V. Net exports and imports are calculated as the difference between production and consumption in the region studied. Flows of trade are then computed in order to minimize transport distances.

To be more precise the model is based on three hypotheses:

(*a*) for each sector, production is supposed to be proportional to the regional employment;

(*b*) there are no net flows between exporting regions or between importing regions;

(*c*) for terminal industries regional consumption is proportional to regional income; for intermediate industries proportional to the regional employment and to the corresponding lines of the inverted national matrix.

The method employed for the Lyon region has been as follows:

(1) determination of the regional production in each sector;

(2) determination of the regional consumption starting from employment data;

(3) determination of net exports and imports;

(4) allocation of the flows of trade through a transport programme.

[17] See J. R. Boudeville: *Mouvements Commerciaux Interrégionaux en France* (Cahiers de l'ISEA, Serie L No. 10, October 1961).

The problem consists in finding the system of distribution with a minimum of transport distances.

Minimize $T = \sum_j \sum_i d_{ij} x_{ij}$

$i =$ 1,2,3—n exporters
$j =$ 1,2,3—m importers.

Admitting that total imports of the State are met by total exports,

$\sum_j x_{ij} = X_i$ a region exports its production;

$\sum_i x_{ij} = M_j$ a region imports its needs;

$X_{ij} \geqslant 0$ flows of goods are positive data.

The problem is classical and easy to solve without complicated computations.[18]

An alternative method   ¶Another method, which gives a better approximation as far as regional and national markets and also exports are concerned, can start from the Cahen-Ponsard direct enquiry which was conducted during 1964 in twenty-eight large towns in France, covering five million workers, in manufacture and tertiary industries, out of a total of 13·6 million.

In all these large towns, excluding Paris, 42 per cent of the manpower was employed in work for the national market. Forty-three per cent worked for the local market and only 15 per cent for the regional market. This suggests that the regional economy is sparsely integrated[19] and that, on average, it is open on the outside world through regional exports in a ratio of 40 per cent of total sales. There is no data concerning imports, but these could be computed by subtracting regional consumption

[18] In the Rhône-Alpes region and for the three main towns only of Lyon, Grenoble, and Saint-Etienne, employment is distributed between the markets as follows: National 50 per cent; Local 40 per cent; and Regional 10 per cent. Considering that this is the best polarized French region, economic regionalities appear very weak and explain in a way the very loose regional economic consensus of the region compared to its local civilian life.

[19] For greater details see Cahiers de l'ISEA, Serie L No. 9—*Modèles Operationnels Régionaux.*

plus exports from regional production. (The main difficulty is that existing data covers only a third of employed workers.)

On this basis a new model could be based on three hypotheses:

(a) for each sector production is supposed to be proportional to the regional employment;

(b) regional production is broken down in two parts, production for regional use and production for external use, entirely determined by the activity of the large towns;

(c) regional consumption is proportional to regional income for terminal industries and to regional production for intermediate industries.

The method would be as follows:

(1) determination of the regional production in each sector;

(2) determination of regional consumption in each sector;

(3) determination of regional imports through the relation, Imports (M) = Exports (X) + Consumption (C) − Production (P);

(4) allocation of the flows of trade through a transport programme.

A shortcoming of the model is that it takes no account of foreign trade. However, this defect is easily remedied if foreign imports and exports are regionally known. It is sufficient to write: Regional Imports (M_R) = Consumption (C) + Regional Export (X_R) + Foreign Exports (X_F) − Foreign Imports (M_F) − Production (P).

The regionalization of foreign trade has been attempted by CNAT. As far as exports are concerned, statistical estimates are based on exporters' cards. Their utilization is made easier owing to the great concentration of the firms working for the world market. Eighty per cent of total exports are made by 5,000 companies and 42 per cent by 290 firms. At this scale it is possible to obtain a breakdown of localized plants and subsidiaries. The study has been achieved for fifteen different sectors. As far as imports are concerned, a proportional breakdown has been accomplished: (1) for *terminal products* in terms of the urban population, corrected by the regional income index; (2) for *energy* on the direct data of the CEREN; (3) for *intermediate products*, in terms of each sector's employment. The figures for 1962 have been established in the twenty-one programming regions. It is hoped that more accurate data for 1963 will cover eighty per cent of French foreign trade.

It is apparent, from what has been said above, that a fair amount of regionalization of national accounts can be arrived at. This is sufficient to establish, without too much expense and for each programming region, a sound approximation of regional accounts, consistent with the national accounting from which they are drawn.

THE AGRICULTURAL COMPLEX

¶A third and last question must be dealt with. Regionalized national accounting can be used to study in each region the basic problems of the agricultural complex. This kind of study will illuminate one of the structural characteristics of underdevelopment, indicate a frame of reference for the economic conversion of regions, and serve, also, as a guide to the study of interregional models as opposed to regionalized ones.

Every *tableau economique* or input-output table may be diversely aggregated, and experience has shown that it can also be approximately triangulated. These two useful techniques will help to explain the differences of connections, hierarchies, and domination existing in different economic structures.

It is helpful, in this matter, to divide the national matrix into two submatrices: (*a*) the agricultural complex and (*b*) the rest of the economy. This division will indicate – following the type of triangulation revealed by our research – the degree of underdevelopment or industrialization of the economy. From this, some important consequences may emerge from the point of view of a policy of growth.

It is necessary, first, to identify the agricultural complex as a triangular matrix,[20] which must be more or less complete in

---

[20] See J. R. Boudeville: Cahiers de l'ISEA, Serie L No. 12, January 1963; and K. A. Fox: *Food and Agricultural Sectors in Advanced Economies in Structural Interdependence* (Edited by T. Barna; Macmillan, New York, 1963).

relation to the type of economy under examination. The developed countries, such as France and the United States, have elaborate and, to a great extent, similar agricultural complexes. These are shown on the table below:

TABLE 6
Agricultural complex in France (1956) and in USA (1947)

France

	5	4	3	2	1
Organic materials and products 5		0·001	0·015		
food process 4	0·032				0·043
leather process 3			0·291		0·006
wood process 2	0·008	0·002	0·010	0·240	
crops and live sktoc 1	0·017	0·458	0·107	0·139	

USA

	4	3	2	1
fibre process 4	0·320	0·004	0·004	0·000
food process 3	0·023	0·207	0·005	0·121
crops 2	0·066	0·113	0·154	0·397
live stock 1	0·024	0·191	—	0·064

Despite diverse economic structures in the two countries, the connections of the two vertical complexes are, in both cases, asymmetric. On the basis of agriculture and stock breeding a hierarchy pyramid of processed products is established. In

G

underdeveloped countries, such as Brazil, Egypt, or India, the same phenomenon is likely to appear with a growing force.

However, the greatest interest of complex analysis lies perhaps in its insertion in the national or regional inter-industrial matrix. It is important to note that in industrialized and in underdeveloped countries two entirely opposite triangulations are the rule, due to the relative position of the agricultural complex and the rest of the economy in the full matrix.

We shall illustrate the position of industrialized countries by looking at the French case.

TABLE 7
Triangulation of the
national matrix
in France (1956)

| | *direct matrix* | | | *inverse matrix* | | | *general case* | |
	agricultural complex	rest of economy		AC	RE		AC	RE
agricultural complex	0·294	0·033	AC	1·444	0·069	AC	*i*	o
rest of economy	0·104	0·322	RE	0·218	1·486	RE	*i*	*i*
	0·398	0·355		1·662	1·555			

The triangulation appears to be clearer on the inverse matrix than on the direct one. This is further confirmed when the sectorial distribution of income and the rate of consumption are taken into account.

This state of affairs becomes entirely different when we study underdeveloped countries, such as India or even Rio Grande do Sul in Brazil.

J. K. Sengupta has found, for India (1960-61), a triangular matrix quite opposite to the ones which we have already examined. Even in the state of Rio Grande do Sul, which is a more developed country, we are confronted with a similar, opposite, disposition.[21]

---

[21] See J. K. Sengupta: 'Models of Agriculture and Industries in Less Developed Economies', in *Structural Interdependence* (Edited by T. Barna; Macmillan, 1963).

	inversed Indian matrix			inversed RGS matrix			general case	
	AC	RE		AC	RE			
AC	1·293	0·215	AC	1·391	0·271		*i*	*i*
RE	0·051	1·311	RE	0·048	1·435		0	*i*

TABLE 8
Triangulation of
national matrix
less-developed
countries

It would appear that in underdeveloped countries, or in the underprivileged regions of large industrialized economies, current political thought on policies of medium term growth should be the reverse of those in the highly industrialized parts of the world. To maintain or improve the French and American current rate of growth the best policy would be to support the agricultural complex. Whereas the Indian or Brazilian rate of growth can be best increased by supporting industrialization.

This could be made more precise if we return once more to the matrices. For example, in France, if exports of the agricultural complex were to increase by one billion, the economic activity of the rest of the economy would have to grow by 417 million. On the other hand, if industrial exports were to increase by the same amount (one billion), the activity of the agricultural complex will increase by 65 million only, i.e. six times less.

In the case of Rio Grande do Sul the position is completely reversed. The corresponding figures are 48 and 271 millions, six times more instead of six times less if an industrial instead of an agricultural policy is adopted.

It follows, therefore, that industrial growth is currently the best policy for underdeveloped countries. This is due to the fact that agriculture does not use much industrial produce, and even the food processing industries or the fibre processing ones are not sufficiently developed.

However, when the agricultural complex is completely modernized it becomes a good 'client' for the rest of the economy and gains a dominating position, as Aujac has successfully shown. Nevertheless, when the industrial sector develops also, in relation to the rest, its weight counteracts the unitary dominant effect of the agricultural complex. In France, for example, the production of the agricultural complex is estimated to be 65 billion francs, which is small compared to the output of the rest of the economy, valued at 207 billion francs. In other words, a 10 per cent increase in agricultural production (6·5 billion) brings about only a 2·7 billion increase in the rest of the economy, or an equivalent of 1·3 *per cent*. On the other hand, a similar (10 per cent) production increase in the rest of the economy is a 20·7 billion growth and brings about a 2 *per cent* (1·33 billion) increase in the agricultural complex.

What we have said is most important for two national economies inside a larger international region; namely for France in the Common Market, whose situation can be contrasted with that of Southern Italy (Mezzogiorno). If these two economies are represented by their two sectorial aggregation matrices, their types of triangulation are transposed (symmetrical). This may be explained by the greater importance that food-and-leather processing industries have in France. It means that in a rural economy the agricultural multiplier is smaller than the industrial one. In countries such as France it is helpful to develop the agricultural complex, while in the Mezzogiorno it is more important to industrialize, even in the agricultural sector. This would increase the Italian agricultural multiplier: the new manufacturing industries will provide the new food processing industries. When a sufficient level of industrialization is reached, the inter-industry matrix will become of the French type.

Regional trade and subsidies ¶In the previous argument we have paid little attention to regional trade and subsidies. This is an important loophole that we should be able to close in the next chapter. It will suffice here to say that if we divide France into two parts – the agricultural West and the industrialized East – and two sectors – the agricultural complex (1) and the rest of the economy (2) we would find a matrix of the following type.

Even with the most important inclusion of distributed sectorial income, and consumption of terminal products, our policy conclusions would remain the same. But we must now turn to autonomous regional development.

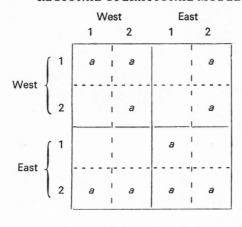

TABLE 9
French West-East
inter-regional
matrix

Regional Operational Models
II: Autonomous Regional Development

Autonomous regional development

¶Autonomous regional development can be considered either as steady growth brought about by previous specialization or as a new and original will to develop; or both. Both methods will create some opposition between regions, within an economy where factors of production are limited. Inevitably, conflicts will arise from this 'oligopolistic competition' which will force the central government to intervene, as the conflict threatens to slow down the rate of growth of the economy as a whole.

Nevertheless, the establishment of additional and competitive enterprises, which would not have existed without local regional initiative, counteracts the constraints imposed by a limited stock of factors of production. Thus, autonomous development should not be regarded as a problem merely of conflict and self-defence between regional groups or organizations; or, again, as one of the new local constraints added to the problem of national 'optimum' growth; it is also a factor which contributes new human and natural resources to the national set. This is why a centralized state is not a pre-condition of attaining the economic optimum. Two problems, therefore, have to be examined: (*a*) how does autonomous regional growth fit into national welfare; (*b*) what sort of arbitration can be designed between the wants and policies of different regions?

REGIONAL GROWTH AND NATIONAL GROWTH

¶Economic growth is not a spontaneous, homogeneous, or

harmonized phenomenon. It appears in dynamic regions, through propulsive sectors, and the overspill effect influences other regions in a variety of different ways. Therefore two types of study are possible: (1) The first (American) method considers the various regions as subsets of given structures and proceeds to study the role of these structures in a given national set. As a result, it prescribes policies favourable to a number of regions. (2) The second (French) method starts with a polarized regional set and aims at developing or preserving its regional radiations by providing the necessary facilities or even by promoting local initiative in a selected number of regions.

¶ These two methods can be successfully illustrated by a number of 'heterogeneous growth' models and by an equal number of 'polarized growth' models.

(a) Heterogeneous growth models

(a) Models of *uniform growth*,[1] where the production of all goods and services evolves at the same constant rate, rely primarily on fixed capital and consumption coefficients and tend towards equilibrium, in the long run (where, indeed, the fundamental hypothesis of fixity is unattainable). Such models are a generalization of the stationary equilibrium. The problem of *balanced growth* may at first appear in the shape of some oscillations around uniform growth, so long as technical and capital coefficients, as well as socio-economic consumption coefficients, remain stable. But these heroic assumptions become questionable as soon as we go further than the five-year period. Development and economic progress, on the other hand, presuppose a substitution of capital for labour, and changes in the proportions of goods which a society desires at any one time. The uniform sectoral growth model, discarding the disparity of regional growth, is therefore utterly unrealistic.

(b) *Harmonized growth*, in the Perroux model (to a greater degree even than in Nurkse's), does not dispense with or ignore technical and psychological innovations. It aims at accelerating the trend; at eliminating the fluctuation; at reducing social tensions between competing economic agents.[2] From the start, for growth to 'take off' and be sustained, the changing com-

[1] R. Solow and P. Samuelson: *Balanced Growth under Constant Returns to Scale* (Econometrica, 1953).
[2] F. Perroux: *L'Economie du XXe Siècle* (PUF 1961).

position of production must adapt itself to the changing composition of demand.[3] The changing composition of the regional supply of factors of production must also adapt itself to the changing demand for regional goods. However, if scarcity of factors of production creates competition between regions, demand (together with its vertical and horizontal connections) will necessitate that regions should be complementary rather than competitive. Such is the basic structure of models describing the changing activities of different sectors of different regions during the growth process.

In our analysis, we shall begin by examining a simple type of interregional model, where the structures are given; where more than two regions are taken into account; and which describes the assistance that must be given to the slow-growing ones. Of all the various models which H. B. Chenery has worked out, the most interesting deal with the transfer problem. In his latest model of the Italian economy, subdivided into three broad regions, he attempts to determine the transfer required to obtain a given regional income growth *per capita*, in the given economic structure; or to find the appropriate means to induce a change of structure in order to allow a similar regional growth without any transfer or increase of transfers. In this model, the emigration factor can be taken into account. In short, it summarizes the current and vital problem of aid from rich to poor regions, which can equally be found in Great Britain, France, Italy, and North America. From this point, a decision model can be built.

This will show, at first, how a given rate of growth in national income will bring about very different rates of increase in each of the three regions. It will also suggest that the remedy could lie in a policy of structural remodelling, and not in one of assistance. Finally, it will show why, in spite of large resource transfers in the form of basic public investment, and of important incentives to the private sector, it has been impossible to palliate, until recently (1961-2), the lack of development in the Mezzogiorno. In effect, the traditional localization of slow-growing sectors in the southern region has not changed. The

[3] R. Nurkse: *Problems of Capital Formation in Underdeveloped Countries* (Oxford, 1955).

southern products are subject to a very low elasticity of income demand compared with those of other regions.

To achieve parity in rates of growth, measured in terms of income *per capita*, a transfer system is necessary. This will create a growing disequilibrium in the 'balance of payments' between regions, which may go on at a rapidly increasing rate. On the other hand, it will make possible the calculation of the minimum structural change which has to take place to offset an increase in the transfers. Chenery computes it to be a 6·5 per cent increase of the manufacturing industries located within the southern region of the country; this, in turn, means that 25 per cent of Italy's industrial investment would have to be concentrated in the Mezzogiorno.

¶ We shall present this most helpful model of Chenery's in nine equations.

The first expression represents planned national economic growth. If θ is the growth rate and P_t is the gross national product in period t, we have:

$$P_t = (1 + \theta)^t P_0 \tag{1}$$

where P_0 refers to the base period.

The second equation expresses the equilibrium position between demand and supply for each sector, assuming a national as well as a regional self-sufficiency in the markets of each product. Thus we call X_{i_N}, X_{i_C}, and X_{i_S} the national market products manufactured in the North, Centre and South respectively. The demand for the products of the national market can be final (D_i) or intermediate (Z_i). Hence the equation will be:

$$X_N + X_C + X_S = D + Z \quad i = (1, 2, 3 \ldots n). \tag{2}$$

Similarly, for each region (r), and for each regional market product (j) we have:

$$X_r = D_r + Z_r \quad j = (1, 2, 3 \ldots m). \tag{3}$$

with $j = i$.

Now, the *structural equations* can also be written separately, for the country as a whole, and for the regions.

The first structural relation describes the supply conditions in the regions (R) and makes the distinction between the proportional effect and the differential effect, i.e. the role played by a region in the sectors of national production and the variation of this role between the years (o) and (t).

$$X_{R_t} = K_{R_0} X_{N_t} + K_{R_t} X_{N_t} \qquad (4)$$

where X_{N_t} is the national market in year (t); K_{R_0} is the quota of the region in year (o) on the national market; K_{R_t} is the variation of the region's part between (o) and (t).

The K_{R_t} will be considered in the model as a policy instrument and not as a test for 'dynamic' development. Therefore, we assume that normal development is proportional.

The second structural relation describes the demand for national market products, which can be subdivided into final demand (D) and intermediate demand (Z). We assume that for each product *final demand* has a constant income elasticity (μ).

$$D_t = D_0 \left(\frac{R_t}{R_0} \right)^{\mu}. \qquad (5)$$

Intermediate demand results from the traditional input-output table which describes the national interindustry relationships.

$$Z_t = A_t X_t. \qquad (6)$$

We assume that the national matrix A_t, is equal to A_0 or that it can be obtained by an equivalent transformation.[4]

When we describe the *structural equations of the regions*, we deal with goods produced and consumed in each region. We shall further assume, for simplicity, that they are final goods, otherwise the national procedure (see equation 6) has to be applied.

Thus a regional demand may be written as follows:

$$D_{rt} = D_{r0} \left(\frac{Y_{rt}}{Y_{r0}} \right)^{\mu} \qquad (7)$$

where Y is the regional resources and μ the income elasticity of the product.

However, regional buying power has a dual origin; first, the added regional values (P_r), and, second, the transfers (T_r) to or from the region

[4] Richard Stone: *Input Output and National Accounts*, O.E.E.C., 1961.

$$Y_r = P_r + T_r. \qquad (8)$$

Once more, T_r is considered to be a policy instrument rather than a variable. Finally, P_r (value added) is of a constant proportion in the sectors of production for all regions.

$$P_r = qX_R, \qquad (9)$$

where (q) is the coefficient for value added.

¶ Chenery's model, or any other similar type, enables us to distribute growth between sectors and regions, provided we possess the input-output national matrix, the income demand elasticities for the various terminal products, the proportional effect coefficients, and the regional transfers which we are allowed to mobilize. However, the model does not take costs into account. It simply indicates desirable directions of industrial growth, without telling us if these are possible, or which is the most appropriate solution, simply because it does not include costs or any polarization effect.

At present, in the Mezzogiorno, the orientation has been towards the path of polarized growth. Industrial concentration is promoted in nine main development areas, covering more than 200,000 people, and in seventeen smaller ones. Moreover, the participation of state industries in the basic sectors such as steel and petrochemicals constitutes a propulsive basis for all other industries in the region. It appears, therefore, that Italy has adopted quite spontaneously the Perrouxian policy of development poles.

¶ Polarized growth models attempt to be more realistic than heterogeneous growth models, whose roots still plunge deep in the wonderland of uniform growth. In an economy which is linked by the processes of industrialization and urbanization, the new models succeed by taking account of the presence of geographic poles and polarized regions; they also highlight the importance which characterizes the concept, in economic development, of a propulsive industry and its associated sectors; finally they make use of this information in estimating the basic investment requirements which the development of propulsive towns must reckon with. In short, polarized growth models

(b) Polarized growth models

attempt to combine the dual objectives of human activity, i.e. the quest for a larger radius of influence and the attainment of greater welfare: in the language of the entrepreneur, a larger volume of sales and a greater profit; in the jargon of a region, enlarged boundaries and higher income *per capita*.

It is true, however, that polarized models make use of the traditional analytical tools which the heterogeneous growth models have provided; yet at the same time they add, to this armoury, new instruments which can be regarded as better adapted to tackle the problems facing the modern world.

We shall begin with the examination of a *boundaries scheme*, and of the *intensity of flows* that a polarized region may possess. Recent research (Hautreux) verified the Isard-Reilly law in its most general formulation. That is, although urban masses may attract themselves proportionately to their population and inversely to the square of their distance, this 'law' does not faithfully represent a gravitation function, but rather an information function, with a more or less elastic distance brake.

It would be more correct to say that two towns, A and B, interchange proportionally to their respective populations, P_a and P_b, and inversely to a stable power of their distance. (In the case of large and diversified metropoles, and for total transactions, this power is equal or very close to two.)

Therefore, if we call the flow, between A and B, $^aX^b$, the Isard-Reilly law for total interchange may be written as follows:

$$^aX^b = K \frac{P_a P_b}{P_a + P_b} \left(\frac{1}{D_{ab}} \right)^2. \qquad \text{(10a)}$$

D_{ab}, the distance between the two towns, is a datum. Total population $(P_a + P_b)$ is described by the denominator. Thus if both populations were to double, the flows between them would not quadruplicate but double in value. We are in the presence of a linear relation which can be introduced easily into our linear models. This fundamental modification was first suggested by Leontief.[5]

[5] W. Leontief and A. Strout: '*Multi-regional Input-Output Analysis*', in *Structural Interdependence and Economic Development* (Edited by T. Barna, Macmillan, 1963). A similar formula was advanced by Pöyhönsen and Pulliainen, the Finnish economists, in EK. Samf. Tidskrift (No. 2), 1963—but without any corrections in the denominator.

But the flows from an agglomeration V, within a distance of D_{va} from pole A, and of D_{rb} from pole B, would according to equation (10a), be distributed in a way giving too small an influence to population. This is:

$$\frac{v_x a}{v_x b} = \frac{P_a}{P_b} \frac{P_v + P_b}{P_v + P_a} \left(\frac{D_{vb}}{D_{va}}\right)^2.$$

Hence, we shall not adopt the Leontief version of Reilly's Law but the classical $^aX^b = KP_aP_b \left(\frac{1}{D_{ab}}\right)^2.$ \hfill (10b)

Thus between regions A and B the borders (D_b), the radius (R_b), and the surface (S_b) of region B are given by:

$$D_b = \frac{D_{ab}}{\sqrt{\dfrac{P_a}{P_b}} + 1} \qquad\qquad D'_b = \frac{D_{ab}}{\sqrt{\dfrac{P_a}{P_b}} - 1} \qquad \text{(11a)}$$

$$R_b = \frac{D_b + D^1_b}{2} \qquad\qquad \frac{D_b + D'_b}{2} \qquad\qquad \text{(11b)}$$

$$S_b = \Pi(R_b)^2 \qquad\qquad \text{(11c)}$$

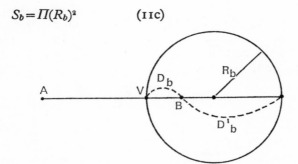

If we have more than two towns, the area under a region will possess borders built from arcs of different circles, which when quantified in terms of the travel time, will take the shape of an irregular bordered regional curve.

The exponent of the Isard-Reilly law is a *distance elasticity*. There are as many different elasticities as there are products. However, it is possible to obtain a total elasticity for aggregate trade, and the total elasticity coefficient between diversified towns is 2. The best general formula for each product i can be written as follows:

$$^aX^b{}_i = K_i W_a P_a W_b P_b \left(\frac{\text{I}}{D_{ab}}\right)^{\pi i}$$

In this formulation W_a and W_b are weights describing diversification of activities in Tables A and B.

Alternative model ¶A slightly different polarized function of trade flows[6] including income elasticities has been deduced, as follows, by Tinbergen, Pöyhönsen, and Pulliainen, almost simultaneously:

$$X_{ij} = C_i C_j \frac{R_i^a R_j^b}{D_{ij}^d}$$

where (i) is the exporting country, (j) the importing one, R_i and R_j their national products, C_i and C_j regionalization coefficients, (a) and (b) income elasticities, and (d) a distance elasticity.

The most important feature of this formula is that exponents (a) and (b) were discovered to be almost equal to one. However, from our dynamic point of view, it is inferior to (10a) and to Leontief's very close formulation. Indeed, inter-urban and international trade could be described as growing like the square of national and world income, which is far from being true. We thus propose to rewrite it thus:

$$X_{ij} = C_i C_j \frac{R_i R_j}{R_i + R_j} \left(\frac{\text{I}}{D_{ij}}\right)^d$$

Notice that Leontief goes still further and takes $d = 1$. But it seems hardly permissible for our purpose to sacrifice to mathematical homogeneity the true significance of our distance brake. As population is of easier statistical access than income, we will often satisfy ourselves with equation (10b).

Thus, for practical reasons, the construction of our polarized models are based on equations (10b) and (11a). Equation (10b)

[6] J. Tinbergen: *Shaping the World Economy* (Twentieth Century Fund, New York, 1962).

J. Waelbroeck: *Le Commerce de la Communauté Européenne avec les Pays Tiers* (Integration Européenne et Réalité Economique, Semaine de Bruges, 1964).

determines the flows between two polarized regions centred round their pole, whereas equation (11a) indicates the population of town B required in order to maintain, or extend, its radius of influence, when competition exists with town A. Equation (11a) shows that if town A were to grow at a given rate (say t_a), town B would also have to grow at the same rate, $t_b = t_a$, to keep its border immutable. Of course, spontaneously this is never the case.

Further, equation (11a) shows that if two towns of different size, B and C, share, with a foreign town, A, the same economic border, F, it is more economic to maintain F, by assisting the smaller town B (which is closer to A) rather than the larger and more distant town C.

Let us take the simplest case, as illustrated by the following diagram, where F is the common economic border of B and C with A.

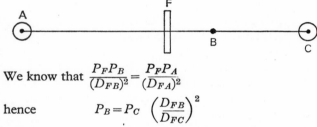

We know that $\dfrac{P_F P_B}{(D_{FB})^2} = \dfrac{P_F P_A}{(D_{FA})^2}$

hence $\qquad P_B = P_C \left(\dfrac{D_{FB}}{D_{FC}}\right)^2$

if this relation holds for increments $\triangle P_B$ and $\triangle P_C$ of the populations of both towns. As B is the smaller and closer town to F, we know that $\dfrac{D_{FB}}{D_{FC}} < 1$, say $\dfrac{1}{3}$ which shows that one additional inhabitant of town B has the same influence on the border F as 9 or $\left(\dfrac{D_{FC}}{D_{FB}}\right)^2$ additional inhabitants of C.

¶ The importance of this problem gains recognition when the abolition of Customs dues is discussed at a common market level. For example, it is almost certain that part of the economic activity generated in the state of Rio Grande do Sul will pass into Uruguayan orbit once the creation of ALALC is fully realized, if the industrialization effort in Pelotas (town B) is not accomplished well in advance.

It is within the frame of the polarized region, described with the help of Reilly's law, that the economic inter-relations are at their maximum and must be studied.

In other words, we must go up one step on the causal scale and explain or plan with the greatest possible efficiency the development of growth poles through the mechanism of their propulsive industries. (The relation between total and active population can be established in each sector or globally through statistical correlation.)

Propulsive ¶ The concept of a growth pole is associated with the notion of
structure propulsive industry. Since we are examining the regional setting and not the national space, it would be preferable to describe poles as a geographic agglomeration of activities rather than as a complex system of sectors different from the national matrix. In short, growth poles will appear as towns possessing a complex of propulsive industries.

A propulsive industry has two characteristics: (a) a direct and indirect dominating influence over all other activities; and (b) an oligopolistic concentration of industry, with price leadership and a keen sense of anticipation in the moves of its own sector as well as in related branches.

The first characteristic can be analyzed in two ways; through the Leontief multiplier effect, and through the polarization effect described by Perroux and Hirschman.[7]

The multiplier effect can be expressed as follows:

$$X = (1 - Ar)^{-1}Y \tag{12}$$

where A is the technical matrix, (r) the diagonal regionalization matrix, and Y the final demand.

For the regions $g = 1, 2, 3$, the matrix can take the following form:

[7] F. Perroux: *La Notion de Pôles de Croissance* (Economie Appliquée, 1955) and L'Economie du XXe Siècle (PUF 1961).
A. O. Hirschman: *The Strategy of Economic Development* (Yale University Press, 1959).
F. Perroux emphasises the positive side of growth poles whereas Hirschman stresses the negative aspect. Hirschman's polarization effect is similar to Myrdal's 'Backwash', while Perroux's concept includes the backwash and *spread*.

	1	2	3	E	
1	Z_1	—	—	E_1	X_1
2	—	Z_2	—	E_2	X_2
3	—	—	Z_3	E_3	X_3
E	M_1	M_2	M_3	—	
	X_1	X_2	X_3		

The key regional industries, in Rasmussen's terminology,[8] are those industries with the largest multiplier. They can be recognized, at a first approximation, by inverting the submatrices:

$$A_g = Z_g X_g^{-1},$$

or, even better still, by the inversion of the entire matrix. The indirect effects on the other regions are shown by the submatrices corresponding to M_1, M_2, and M_3, which also indicate the direct and indirect import coefficients. It is possible to integrate, within the matrix, a vector of incomes distributed and another vector of propensity to consume.

Empirical evidence has shown that key regional industries differ between regions. They are set in different internal structures (Z) and possess different openings (M). Moreover, key regional industries (Z) are not necessarily key national industries ($Z+M$). In other words, a basic industry is not always a key industry in a region. Moreover, the multiplier effect is in terms of the unit of production. It does not take account of the size of the industry which, in that case, should be weighted by the size of actual output, thus giving us a percentage instead of a per unit multiplier.

¶ We shall now turn to the *polarization effect*. This has been explained, as we have seen, by Perroux, Youngson, and Hirschman. In short, it states that the increase in the output of a pro-

Polarization effect

[8] P. N. Rasmussen: *Studies of Intersectoral Relations* (North-Holland Publishing Co., 1956).

H

pulsive industry may induce the creation of other activities not yet localized in the region. This is achieved by three different mechanisms: upstream, downstream, and lateral. Let us begin with the upstream mechanism.

The establishment or increase in production of a propulsive industry will induce the manufacture of inputs required in the main activity. In a sense this will lead to the basic idea of the multiplier, except that it would, to begin with, leak into imports. When shall there be import substitution? To answer this it is important to have some knowledge about the dispersion of the inputs of the buying activity. Indeed a large number of diversified small purchases (direct or indirect) will most probably have no influence on regional localization of new firms because of the *minimum economic size* of the seller.

We may use in that respect the Rasmussen coefficient δ_j, which measures the dispersion of inputs,[9] in other words, the concentration. The smaller δ_j is, the smaller the concentration and the greater the probability of the polarization impact through the creation of new industries. Therefore it seems useful to weight the multiplier effect by the concentration index in order to classify polarizing industries.

$$\Pi j = m_j \delta_j \text{ where } m_j \text{ is the multiplier } \sum_i b_{ij} \text{ of the inverted}$$

matrix (13a)

$$\Pi_j = n\mu_j \delta_j \text{ where } \mu_j \text{ is the mean } \frac{1}{n} \sum_i b_{ij} \text{ of column } j \quad (13b)$$

A very similar method, though in a different fashion, has been advanced by A. O. Hirschman. He makes the clearest contrast between the *importance* of the linkage effect (Rasmussen's u_j) and the *probability* for sellers to receive an initial stimulus (Rasmussen's δ_j).

He proposes for the second phenomenon the following and simpler measure: 'Suppose industry W requires annual inputs

[9] If we call μ_j the mean of the n coefficients of the column j of the inverted matrix $(\mathrm{I} - A)^{-1} = B$ of order n, we obtain

$$\delta_j = \sqrt{\frac{1}{n} \sum (\mu_j - b_i b_{ij})^2}.$$

However, this concentration index being awkward, Rogers' index may be preferred.

of Y_1, Y_2, and Y_3, and that the minimum economic size of firms that would turn out this input is equal to a_1, a_2, a_3. Then the strength of the stimulus, or the probability that the setting up of industry W will generate on industries producing the inputs, is equal to the ratio of the $Y's$ to the $a's$.'[10] His formula could therefore be written as follows:

$$P_W = \sum_i^n X_i P_i \qquad (13c)$$

where X_i is the direct input which would take the place of b_{ij}, and P_i the place of δ_j, in (13a). $P_i = \dfrac{Y_i}{a_i}$ is the probability of the creation of industry (i).

From the regional point of view, we would have to make sure that these regional inputs and labour supply are still adequate for the new industry; as well as to consider how favourable the comparative costs are.

¶ We shall now examine the *forward linkage*. We begin with the special but limited case which Hirschman called *satellite industry*. As principal inputs, these industries use the output of the propulsive industry. They derive an important locational advantage from its proximity. Moreover, these satellite industries have a smaller minimum economic size. If these three conditions are satisfied, the polarization becomes highly probable; when they are not fulfilled, polarization is more haphazard. For example, a cement factory can easily lead to the establishment of a brick works; steel works can lead to the establishment of tube manufacture; but the same steel works does not necessarily induce mechanical industries. It is traditional in this field to contrast the integrated Ruhr, the less integrated Limbourg, and French Lorraine, which possesses only steel works.

This stems from the fact that the principal supplier of the polarized industry is not the propulsive firm, and that the *minimum economic size* of the induced manufacture is frequently as large as that of the propulsive one. Such is the case in the motor car industry. Finally, locational advantages other than supply proximity may be important; such as the market.

Satellite industry and forward linkage

[10] A. O. Hirschman: *The Strategy of Economic Development*, p. 101.

This analysis brings us to the study of industrial complexes dominated simultaneously by the concepts of market, and of minimum economic size. Of course the joint creation of inter-related industries increases their potential for joint polarization. Such manufactures could be thought of as a 'development block'. They form a submatrix in which the minimum economic sizes of the joint industries induce a total internal consumption equal, say, to half of each one's output, the remaining half being given to the market. This may be expressed by the following submatrix:

$$
\begin{bmatrix}
- & a_{jk} & a_{jl} \\
a_{kj} & - & a_{kl} \\
a_{lj} & a_{lk} & -
\end{bmatrix}
\times
\begin{bmatrix}
c_j \\
c_k \\
c_l
\end{bmatrix}
=
\begin{bmatrix}
\frac{c_j}{2} \\
\frac{c_k}{2} \\
\frac{c_l}{2}
\end{bmatrix}
$$

or by the following equation:

$$
\sum_s a_{rs} c_s = \frac{1}{2} c_r \quad \begin{matrix} r = (j \dots l) \\ s = (j \dots l). \end{matrix}
$$

An industrial complex, comprising, let us say, steel (j), car (k) and electronics (l) industries may be called a polarization vector, e.g. c_j, c_k and c_l, representing minimum capacity. This vector could be determined through a spatial correlation coefficient between states or regions; and whenever possible through a time correlation, taking account of location, and associated with regional growth.

Lateral effect is mostly associated with the availability of labour and with social overhead capital. In Youngson's terms 'initiatory investment' is enlarged by 'long-period growth investment'.[11] A good example of this effect is given by Matilla and Boudeville on residential investment,[12] which brings us

[11] A. J. Youngson: *Possibilities of Economic Progress*.
[12] J. R. Boudeville: *Note sur l'Implantation des Industries—Clés dans la Région Rhône-Alpes* (Annales de l'Université de Lyon, 1958).
Matilla: *Review of Economics and Statistics*, November 1956.

back to our starting point, namely the population increase of towns.

Another way of estimating polarization effect is to look backward through time. Assuming that technical coefficients are precise, and constant, it would be easy to separate the multiplier effect and the polarization effect in the total evolution through time. We could write: polarization effect = total evolution minus multiplier effect. Given matrix A_t, at time (t), with some key sectors (i.e. car and electronics industries) not in existence at time $(t-1)$ we know that:

$$X_t = A_t X_t + Y_t = (1 - A_t)^{-1} Y_t$$

If we take away from Y_t, the sectors s (car and electronics) we then have:

$$(1 - A)_t^{*-1}(Y_t - Y_s) = X_t^*$$

where $A^* = A$ minus lines and colums (s).

X_t^* is the production which should have existed at price t in the period $t - 1$, everything else remaining unchanged except for the sectors (s). The difference $X_t - X_t^*$ is the pure multiplier effect, say M. But, in fact, production during the period $(t-1)$, even revalued at (t) period prices X_{t-1}^*, is not X_t^*. It is smaller and this increased difference $X_t^* - X_{t-1}^*$, is the polarization effect P. Indeed $X_t - X_{t-1}^* = M + P$.

Alas, there is the possibility that the difference could stem from a change in technical coefficients. Moreover, the difference could largely be due to the consequence of statistical deficiencies of the model.[13] We are inclined to concentrate on the previous method.

¶ For each activity effect it is possible to tally a price effect. The cost effect is in a way the transposed multiplier effect. External economies are the transposed polarization effects. However, the price effect is also linked to oligopolistic structure of production, giving to the propulsive firms a real, dominant, influence on prices. This point may be one of the conditions reflecting minimum economic size. Price domination opens the possibility of self-financing, particularly of research which may lead to the

Oligopolistic concentration

[13] S. Lombardini, Ires, Italconsult, and Sema: *Structure et Perspectives Economiques d'une Region* (Torino), Milan, 1962.

creation of new products. (Expenditure in University teaching, in a given region, has a similar effect. It will increase the probability of innovations in that sector.) However, here we are only concerned with an activity model and not a price model.

A polarization activity model   ¶With the tools already discussed several polarization models can be constructed.[14]

Consider the one we have already used, for the State of Rio Grande do Sul. This particular model is made up of three regions, polarized by Montevideo with a population of 1,211,000 Porto Alegre (618,000), and Pelotas (121,000); these regions come very close to the existing political boundaries. The elimintion of customs will place the States of Uruguay and Rio Grande do Sul under the free international influence of polarization.

The first problem, for the State of Rio Grande do Sul, is to make sure that the economic border coincides with the political line of demarcation. The second problem is to bring about the maximum welfare of the Brazilian regions. Generally, the problem can be formulated as follows: let (A) be Montevideo, (B) Pelotas, and (C) Porto Alegre. The polarized economic borders of Pelotas and Porto Alegre, while in competition with Montevideo for the construction of a direct coastal highway, can be given by:

$$D_{FB} = \frac{D_{AB}}{1 + \sqrt{\dfrac{P_A}{P_B}}}$$

$$D_{FC} = \frac{D_{AC}}{1 + \sqrt{\dfrac{P_A}{P_C}}}$$

Let Q_B and Q_C be the distance between the *political* border and towns B and C. For the political and economic borders to coincide, the populations of town B and C must amount to:

[14] J. Paelinck: *La Teoria del Desarollo Regional Polarisado* (Revista de Economia Latino-Americana, Caracas, 1963).
J. R. Boudeville: *Croissance Polarisée du Rio Grande do Sul* (Mimeographed).
J. A. Bermejo: *Rejacoes Interindustriais no Estado do Rio Grande do Sul*, 1953, Porto-Alegre, 1958.

$$P_B = P_A \left(\frac{Q_B}{Q_A}\right)^2$$

$$P_C = P_A \left(\frac{Q_C}{Q_A}\right)^2$$

Regional structures: On the whole, the Pelotas region is a rural one. Its simplified matrix (aggregated in two sectors: the agricultural complex[15] and the rest of the economy) has the triangular form of an underdeveloped region.

In this agricultural region the activities with the highest multiplier are industrial.

The developed region of Porto Alegre is mainly secondary and tertiary. Its matrix is of the type:

There the activities with high multiplier will be found in the agricultural complex. Thus it would seem that what the Pelotas-Rio Grande region needs is an industrial complex, which would form a growing and prosperous conurbation, while an agricultural complex would help to develop the polarized region of Porto Alegre. So far our reasoning has neglected an important factor, namely the interregional connections.

¶ In our model we deal with three regions, two of which – Montevideo and Porto Alegre – are of the developed industrial type, and one – Pelotas – is of the underdeveloped agricultural type.

Inter-regional connections

[15] The agricultural complex includes food and fibre processing industries.

They exchange two types of goods: food stuffs (natural or processed) X_1, and manufactured industrial goods X_2. The interregional flow of goods coming from region A and going to region B is given by equations of the following type:

$$^AX_1^B = K_1 P_A P_B \left(\frac{1}{D_{ab}} \right)^{\pi_1}$$

$$^AX_2^B = K_2 P_A P_B \left(\frac{1}{D_{ab}} \right)^{\pi_2}$$

where P_A and P_B stand for total population of A and of B; exponent π_1 is the food distance-brake; and exponent π_2 is the industrial distance-brake. Both may be easily obtained by the cartographic border method pioneered in Lyon, by means of regression analysis. Its utilization is linked with the availability of data.

If we call U_i^A the total production of industry i in region A, the coefficient $^BX^i\ U_i^A$ may be computed and supposed stable as an import (input) coefficient. Hence it is possible to draw an interregional matrix for the Rio Grande do Sul. The problem is then to invert a square matrix of order 6 (2 sectors and 3 regions) so that we can discover the sector with the highest interregional multiplier, with regard to Pelotas and Porto Alegre. The resultant sub-matrix can be drawn as follows:

Inverted interregional Matrix

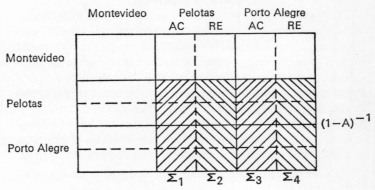

This matrix shows the four vertical totals of the coefficients of two sectors (agricultural complex, rest of the economy) in the south-east of the matrix.

It is worth while stressing that instead of the classical inversion, indicating direct and indirect supplies necessary to satisfy final demand, it is often more interesting to know the supplies required to satisfy *final or intermediary* demand. Therefore, it is necessary to divide the column of coefficients in the inverted matrix $(\mathrm{I} - A)^{-1}$ by the corresponding term of the diagonal of the same matrix $(\mathrm{I} - \overset{\frown}{A})^{-1}$.

¶ We began with the existing structure in a region and must now consider its possible modifications. The industrialization of the agricultural region will not be accomplished by the multiplication of small cottage industries and old manufactures; new factories must be established. This industrialization, moreover, will have an overspill effect in the form of a modernized agricultural complex, e.g. food processing industries. The problem becomes one of choice between sets of connected investment having their own technical coefficients. *Propulsive industries and mutations of structure*

Assume the introduction of a mechanical electronic complex in Rio Grande do Sul and that we hesitate in the choice of location as between Pelotas (*B*) and Porto Alegre (*C*). We would establish, in effect, a set of new products in one or the other region. This complex could be treated as a new sector, added to rest of the economy. Or, suppose that we hesitate over the expense of introducing a new type of culture, a new agricultural complex, in one or the other region.

Both problems can be dealt with through linear programming. Instead of two sectors per region, we now count four. The constraint of a minimum population for Pelotas has to be added. The objective could be a minimum capital expenditure. The main difference from the previous schema is that we conceive of a given global demand for each product. Indeed, this demand could be estimated through the previous schema.

The model can therefore be formalized in the following way. We have four products, two for each region, and eight production functions, four in each region. The supply of each product should be at least equal to demand. Industrial employment (E_B) of region B should create an agglomeration of population in town (B) at least equal to the minimum requirement. Invested capital should be minimum.

Capital coefficients are given. The hypothesis is that additional industrial employment accrues in the region, to the metropolis and its conurbation.

Let the activities be $X_1 \ldots X_8$ $(j = 1 \ldots 8)$.

Let the product be P_1, P_2, P_3, P_4 $(i = 1 \ldots 4)$, and their total demand D_1, D_2, D_3, D_4.

Let technical coefficients be $-a_{ij}$ for inputs and 1 for outputs.

Let labour coefficients for X_3, X_4 of region B be m_3, m_4.

Let industrial employment of region B be E_B.

Let the capital coefficients be $K_1 \ldots K_8$.

We can construct the following matrix:

	Region B				Region C				Demand
	CA		RE		CA		RE		
	X_1	X_2	X_3	X_4	X_5	X_6	X_7	X_8	
Product P_1 CA	1	0	$-a_{13}$	$-a_{14}$	1	0	$-a_{17}$	$-a_{18}$	$\geqslant D_1$
P_2	0	1	$-a_{23}$	$-a_{24}$	0	1	$-a_{27}$	$-a_{28}$	$\geqslant D_2$
Product P_3 RE	$-a_{31}$	$-a_{32}$	1	$-a_{34}$	$-a_{35}$	$-a_{36}$	1	$-a_{38}$	$\geqslant D_3$
P_4	0	$-a_{42}$	0	1	0	$-a_{46}$	0	1	$\geqslant D_4$
Labour	0	0	m_3	m_4	0	0	0	0	$\geqslant E_B$
Objective	K_1	K_2	K_3	K_4	K_5	K_6	K_7	K_8	Minimum

The drawback of such a model is that it will tend to favour the activities with the smallest capital coefficients, i.e. the less mechanized and possibly the less profitable. Thus it is more interesting to introduce capital coefficients in the matrix under the form of a constraint ($\leqslant$), and to have for objective the maximum of added value (sales minus material costs of production). The presentation only would be more complex, the solution of the problem remaining essentially the same.

We could introduce other constraints such as the absence of deterioration in the situation of the poorest region (B) in relation to a richer region (C). For example, the rate of growth of production in (B) would be set higher than the rate of growth of production in (C). This can easily be formalised.

Let C_i be the cost of total production from sector X_i, at the end of the planned period. Let X_{0i} be the same activity during the reference period. Let $X_1 \ldots X_4$ be the activities of region (B) and $X_5 \ldots X_8$ be the activities of region (C).

As we said earlier, X_2 and X_4 are new activities in region (B), X_6 and X_8 are new activities in region (C).

We then may write as follows:

$$\frac{C_1 X_{t1} + C_2 X_{t2} + C_3 X_{t3} + C_4 X_{t4}}{X_{01} + X_{03}} -$$
$$\frac{C_5 X_{t5} + C_6 X_{t6} + C_7 X_{t7} + C_8 X_{t8}}{X_{05} + X_{07}} \geqslant 0.$$

This means that the rate of growth in region (B) minus the rate of growth in region (C) must be superior or equal to zero.

These interregional comparisons will lead us to the concept of regional arbitration through income and activity distribution.

ARBITRATION BETWEEN REGIONS

¶Arbitration at national level is a necessity because, in a world of imperfect competition, what is best for the nation is not necessarily the summation of what is best for the regions. Perfect mobility of labour and capital, which would be one of the conditions of perfect competition, would drain away from some regions all their factors of production. It is not sufficient to state that comparative growth constraints must be included. It is necessary to specify which ones, and what is the relevant objective to maximize.

For each objective setting for every arbitration on constraints, we postulate a criterion and hence a value judgment. The combination of several criteria will only add a new value judgment to each of the existing ones: i.e. the choice of weighting. Therefore to search for the minimum of contradictions in the solutions obtained by each and all the criteria is not adequate.[16] The danger stems from the fact that the objectives are composite; the

---

[16] It presupposes an equal weighting of contradictions.

preference function of one region is different from another one; and there is no spontaneous interregional ordering which can emerge. The will of the fittest is not always the best solution to our problem. In this case, the national will must prevail.[17]

Finally, even if one were to admit that a common criterion exists (say, the quest for maximum value added) regional interrelations show that the key industry in a region has no reason to coincide with the national one. We will illustrate the two fundamental causes which contribute towards the divorce of interest between regions.

Differences of value judgment (objective function)

¶ Let us apply the optimum and linear programming theory to the location of activity in Scotland (R_1) and in England (R_2) with only one constraint to production, in mobility of capital. Production is measured in gross national product (GNP_1) (GNP_2). We suppose that, at the beginning, productivity is less in region 1 (Scotland) than in region 2 (England). We suppose, also, that thresholds exist under which capital does not migrate but stays embodied in the land and produces in one region a minimum GNP (say p_a and p_b) and, in the other, a maximum GNP (say P_A and P_B).

*Short term choice
between two regions*

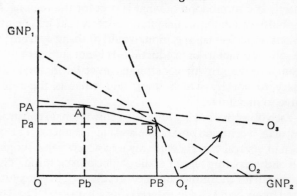

[17] One must not make any confusion between the administrative will of the capital city, and the government of the nation. The creation of Washington and Brasilia tried to prevent such a danger.

The fact that productivity is less in region 1 than in region 2 is pictured by a slope of AB inferior to 45%. A transfer of capital from region 1 to region 2 increases GNP_2 more than it decreases GNP_1. The possible production contour is thus (PA, A, B, PB).

Investment will be guided by our objective function. Provided that it is neutral, £1,000 invested in Scotland means effectively the same as £1,000 invested in England. The slope of the objective function is 45% (function o_2) and the optimum point is B. If we favour England (objective function o_1), the result is the same. If we favour Scotland strongly (objective function o_3) the result is A. Thus our preference function has to have a slope lower than AB, to obtain a maximum Gross National Product in Scotland. For example, a Scottish entrepreneur may feel that external diseconomies are linked with London's traffic glut, and provide for a source of cost increase and that, in any event, the location rents are inequitable.

Moreover, long-term and short-term production possibilities and objective choices are different. In the production plans of the government, the growth of London threatens a severe thrombosis of social productivity so that, from a collective point of view, employment of resources in London becomes less and less productive.

On the other hand, so far as *objectives* are concerned, the government can see all the social and economic disadvantages associated with the underdeveloped vacuum emerging in the Scottish Highlands, and will therefore favour Scotland, inasmuch as it grows poorer in comparison with England. The objective function has a declining slope with time. Thus the long-term view will change the policy entirely. Hence the public interest, in France, in 'Aménagement du Territoire', where the planning bureau has a prospective view (o_2). This takes note of the possibility that maximum productivity in relation to the location of mobile resources (capital or labour) may not correspond to the *short-term* judgment (o_1), which the entrepreneurs or the workers may advocate.

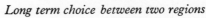

Long term choice between two regions

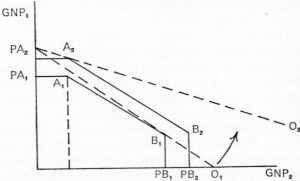

Increase in total resources

¶ The previous model supposes that in every period resources are limited. It was only by passing from period 1 to period 2 that the disposable stock of resources increased exogenously. It is, however, interesting to study how a national policy favourable to the less productive and less advanced region can increase national resources in a more efficient way than through assistance to the more productive one.

Interregional economic relations may be understood in three ways.

(1) There may be peaceful competition for the allocation of limited resources such as capital and labour, the instrument of competition being a low cost of production. But domination effects on prices, income and expectation become rapidly apparent, and as underdeveloped countries and regions become increasingly self-aware, competition degenerates into conflict.

(2) There may be, secondly, a kind of cold war, the objects of which are; to grow at the *expense* of some other region, and, at the same time, to prevent it doing the same. The problem, here, is no longer to produce at low cost in order to sell on a larger market, but to fight the willingness of the other region to buy at low prices and to sell at high ones. This is the famous *terms of trade* conflict.

(3) There is, thirdly, the interchange of techniques, knowledge, ideas, and ideologies, which might well constitute the most important factor in the processes of world economic

development.[17a] Migrations, which for so long were one of the greatest means of intellectual interchange, might prove to be in only a very temporary phase of recession at present. The empty lands of Africa and South America may soon provide testimony of recovery of the old migration trend.

Unfortunately it is well known that competition brings concentration faster than complementarity, and domination by the large international firm[18] faster than economic specialization between nations. Also, economic conflict creates unproductive utilization of resources, highlighted by Haavelmo's[19] strategies of 'grabbing'; protection and even cooperation being mostly directed towards hampering the productive efforts of other groups and to a reduction in global output. Again, international migrations often have an imperialistic trend. In such conditions, one may ask if brakes on economic growth do not become predominant as soon as underdeveloped regions enter into competition or conflict with developed regions, in order to escape from their economic influence.

There are two answers to these questions: the propagation of technical innovation and the challenge and response processes. Both in fact are interdependent.

The most important answer is to be found in the interregional propagation of economic innovation and even in the conditions of its creation. It is significant that the two world wars have been the periods of greatest advance in technical progress. The action of governmental research organizations was prodigiously accelerated. The organization of scientific research and dissemination of its results, as a means of economic or technical advance, is a powerful weapon of our age, but belongs in the realm of the larger firm and of the State. Political and economic warfare provide one of the main stimuli to research. Though they hamper the creation of capital, they increase the level of know-how. This is why they are productive.

[17a] F. Perroux: *Propagation de l'Information dans l'Economie du XXè Siècle* (PUF, 1961), p. 361 and 376.

[18] M. Bye: '*La Grande Unité Internationale*', in *L'Univers Economique et Social, Encyclopédie Française*, tome IX.

[19] T. Haavelmo: *Economic Evolution* (North-Holland Publishing Co., 1954). See the Strategies of Grabbing, Protection, and Cooperation, p. 91.

But it is not enough to oppose productive and unproductive efforts, it is necessary to measure, and to determine the conditions under which the initiatives and organizations created by conflict exceed the brakes and losses, which are easier to detect. The European policy of scientific research, in the sectors of steel and coal, could be a useful field of study. But the main difficulty is to single out which productive efforts were the result of a conflict, in the sense that they would not have existed in its absence.

One must bear in mind that there are three possible responses to a challenge: apathy and submissiveness, constructive activity, and random aggressiveness.[20] The first and third reactions are destructive. The second is the only productive one. Thus the result rests on the mentality and the organization of the regional group. On the other hand, two types of conflict exist. First, there is the conflict of borders between two groups which do not overlap, and are contiguous. Examples of these are international and interregional conflicts, such as exist between firms for market areas. The second type of conflict concerns interpenetrating groups in the same region or space. This is what Boulding calls an *ecological conflict*. Examples are to be found in the religious and racial fields. They are mostly destructive, and we will not study them, so that we may concentrate on the creative aspect of border conflict.

One point, touching on the division between border conflict and ecological conflict, should have light cast on it. The clique conflicts are as destructive as random aggressiveness. A good example can be found in South American social behaviour. The Latin American system of the *Caudillo* rests on a group, or rather a clique, represented and led by its charismatic leader. Characteristic of this is the social egoism of the organized group, working for its own ends rather than for common welfare, and the resulting authoritarian and unstable social climate. To be aggressive and to be organized is quite different from being creative. But, of course, it is better than being apathetic and anarchic. After this little bit of common sense, let us return to border conflict.

[20] K. Boulding: *Conflict and Defense* (Harper Torchbooks, 1963).

¶ Between nations, these conflicts concern tariffs and economic warfare. Between regions, they find expression mainly in contests for the construction of roads, railways and airports, and in the competition to obtain subsidies from the central government. In a previous study on a new approach to international trade in the South-East,[21] I tried to sketch a *krieg-spiel* where the objectives of the adversaries differed and the sum of outcomes was other than zero. The objectives were (1) the accumulation of exchange reserves, (2) the amelioration of the conditions of trade, (3) the increase of employment, (4) the polarization of the largest possible zone of influence. The two first objectives can be studied through a zero sum game. They can also be treated as constraints in a programming model. This is a way of stressing that they are non-productive. On the contrary, full employment through the exports multiplier is a productive target. The same is true for the polarization target and the growth of industrialized poles. Both have to be included in a non-zero sum game. Anyhow the problem is to determine the pay-off matrix. This is the role of our former models.

Social overhead capital

In order to put all available activity potential and human resources at the disposition of the regional or national community, one must eliminate unproductive efforts (accumulation of reserves and price wars) in favour of creative activities (industrial employment). This is, for underdeveloped regions, a problem of social mutation linked with the opening of communications, and the development of public education. Social overhead capital may thus have a far greater effect on productivity than that part that is directly computable. In small agricultural and slow-growing regions, it is necessary to assist the local governments in such policies whenever suitable. Indeed they have to participate in large overhead expenditures and, in France at least, most of the taxes linked with the new activities accrue to the State. A reform of local taxation is one of the clues to the concentration of industries in the principal regional metropolitan areas.

[21] J. R. Boudeville: *Vers une Analyse Nouvelle des Echanges dans le Sud-Est Asiatique* (Cahiers de l'ISEA, Série L No. 9).

I

Choice of regional
objectives

¶When numerous autonomous centres have to choose between various economic policies, two problems arise: the first is to determine the objectives, the second is to find the means.

It is customary to begin with the simplest form, i.e. the choice and measure of means, before considering the choice ordering and weighting of aims. But this is merely to set aside, at the outset, the most important part of the problem, and to assume that only one objective or welfare function exists, by which integration is to be judged. In fact, there are numerous goals and tables of value. In accordance with the German school of '*Leitbild*',[22] we propose to start from the choice of objectives before selecting the means. Therefore we will study (1) integration and the multiplicity of goals, and, later, (2) integration and the multiplicity of political instruments.

Integration and
multiplicity of
goals

¶Economic policy is formulated by a large number of decision centres and is determined by a process of conflict between them, within a set of decision makers who are likely to be more or less integrated.

We can define the integration of a programming region as the convergence of aims (optimum point) and a compatibility of constraints (admissible points). We shall deal only with the first characteristic.

In fact, there exists a multiplicity of goals, and the preference functions of the regions may be so different that no coherent ordering appears to exist at the level of the national or supranational set. This problem of plurality and ordering, the necessity of a concerted dialogue and of an arbitration, is the first and fundamental aspect of integration.

Let us examine why we have to deal with a wide variety of objectives. We have already stressed the possibility of aiming either at the largest radius of *influence* (polarization or sales), or at the highest possible level of *welfare* (income *per capita* or profit). One can also look forward to greater *equality* in the distribution of regional income, and to maintaining and *employing all the regional labour* on its native soil (full regional employment). Numerous variants may be found for all these objectives,

---

[22] Erich Dittrich: *Zum Begriff des Leitbildes in der Diskussion über Raum ordnung* (Information des Instituts für Raum Forschung, 1958).

which can be contradictory even in terms of a single region. Thus maximum added value per employed worker may be in contradiction with full employment in the region, and may lead to emigration. Conversely, maximum added value has little significance if commuters come from other regions (Liège) or more often if the owners of capital are from abroad (Venezuela). Moreover, maximum national productivity necessitates an increase in the mobility of resources, by sector and by region: hence this widespread instability will be resented by workers demanding professional and *regional stability*.

It is not possible in a decision model or in current economic policy to take account of *every* possible aim. One has to choose a limited set constituting the objective function of the programme. To determine this function, one has to express each goal as a function of the other goals; that is to say, it becomes necessary to weight each one, to find a common measure, a sort of price system for the different objectives.

Thus we are once again confronted with the difficult problem of weighting. A weighting system is essentially transitive. To be able to establish one, it seems practical to start from a simple ordering which is as permanent as possible, and to find the weighting giving the same classification and compatible with empirical ranges of variation.

These apparently abstract considerations will enable us to tackle the double and unsolved problem of the plurality of decision centres and of the plurality of criteria known as the *Condorcet paradox*.

¶ Take three regions R_1, R_2, R_3, judging by reference to three criteria *a*, *b*, *c*, but giving them different ordering. Is it possible to find a common ordering; in other words, to integrate the criteria? Is it possible to find some sort of convergence for the different scales of values and even a system of weighting hence the collective order is established? This is a special aspect of the Condorcet problem.

The Condorcet problem

The Condorcet problem for three regions (sectors or groups) is easily represented through a triangular, one-way oriented, graph.

This graph expresses three orderings of criteria abc through circular permutation. Starting from each summit,

For R_1 $a > b > c$
For R_2 $b > c > a$
For R_3 $c > a > b$.

Indeed it may be read either (and simultaneously)

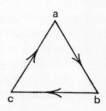

as $\begin{cases} a > b \\ b > c \\ c > a \end{cases}$ or as $\begin{cases} b > c \\ c > a \\ a > b. \end{cases}$

If we adopt the logic rule of transitivity, we stumble upon contradictions. For example, for region R_1 criterion a is more important than criterion c $(a > c)$ through transitivity, but for R_2, $c > a$. In the same way, for R_2 criterion b is more important than criterion c, but for R_3, $c > b$. Lastly, for R_1, $a > b$ and for R_2, $b > a$. To find a solution let us vote. The majority $R_1 + R_3$ imposes the rule $a > b$. Another majority $R_2 + R_3$ imposes the rule $c > a$. Hence through transitivity $c > b$. But a third majority $R_1 + R_2$ imposes the rule $b > c$. The situation is inextricable and contradictory. No collective ordering appears.

On the contrary, it is possible to approximate to a common classification through the technique of domination matrices which sets aside the rule of transitivity. Of course, at first sight, the problem seems hopeless as the matrix associated with the graph is circular and periodic.[23]

Let A be the direct domination associated with graph No. 1. Let us compute indirect (or second degree) domination through an intermediate criterion. We find the matrix A^2 corresponding to the reversed graph.

The domination of fourth degree A^4 gives us back the matrix A. Thus the process is not converging but cyclical; the Condorcet paradox remains unsolved.

But happily it is easy to find a solution to this difficulty. For indeed we will not change the ordering of the criteria in any way if we suppose that there exists a fourth one breaking up the

[23] C. Berge: *La Theorie des Graphes* (Dunod).

Graph 1 and Matrix A

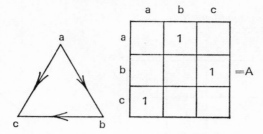

Graph 2 and matrix A^2

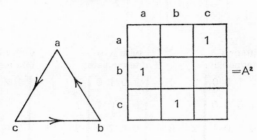

Graph 3 and matrix A^4

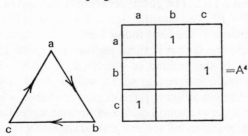

circularity of the graph; which, in practice, it will always be possible to find. In other words we want to show; that, if we agree to take the advice of an arbiter, say the State, and to add a fourth criterion, the solution is always possible.

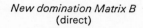

New domination Matrix B
  (direct)

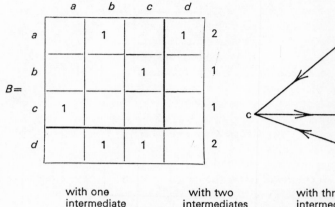

	with one intermediate				
$B^2=$	0 1 2 0	3
	1 0 0 0	1
	0 1 0 1	2
	1 0 1 0	2

	with two intermediates	
$B^3=$	2 0 1 0	3
	0 1 0 1	2
	0 1 2 0	3
	1 1 0 1	3

	with three intermediates	
$B^4=$	1 2 0 2	5
	0 1 2 0	3
	2 0 1 0	3
	0 2 2 1	5

We will easily find that the ordering of criteria stabilizes as soon as the fourth round. The global ordering is the sum of matrices $B + B^2 + B^3 + B^4$. The classification is $a = 13$, $c = 9$, $b = 7$. It will be left unchanged. We have found a common ordering.

¶ The conclusion is that if three regions are quite incapable of agreeing on the ranking of objectives, a fourth region, or better, the State, intervening with a weight equal to the other regions and with a different point of view, will always be able to make them agree at a round table and without any enforcement. We thus at length arrive at a unique and collective classification based on the hypothesis that a direct and indirect preference have the same weight.

But another problem exists. Starting from a common and

agreed ranking, we have to find a cardinal measure offering a possibility of expressing these different objectives in common terms, in order to find an optimum for the group of regions. Thus a weighting has to be found in empirical intervals of variations. Here the role of the fourth party – the State – seems to be even more important. It seems that the Round Table, having given its general ordinal directives, has to leave it to the President to present a small number (e.g. 3) of alternative weightings on which the same type of decision could be taken.

It appears from the start that the role given to the arbitrator assumes the existence of a central government and of a large delegation of powers to its regional representative. This is what is called, in France, 'administrative deconcentration'. From a more general point of view, it appears also that a common table of values demands the existence of a strong executive power. In the last chapters, we shall study, in a more detailed fashion and on an empirical basis, the usage, in France, of these theoretical instruments of 'concerted' regional planning.

The Fourth French Plan

¶ Fully to understand French regional planning, it is necessary to become familiar with the Fourth French Economic Plan (January 1, 1962, to December 31, 1965). This contains the new economic principles known as *prospective* and *concerted economy*, which it gradually introduces at the level of the programming region. In France, the second half of the twentieth century is an era of pragmatic and prospective planning. Economic Science is not just an endeavour towards impartial prevision and unbiased description; it is also a tool, a means of defining a goal and of reaching it at the lowest cost. In Great Britain, as in France, there is now a shift of mental attitude. This is largely due to the influence of three men: Gaston Berger,[1] the philosopher of prospective; François Perroux,[2] who is its main economist; and Pierre Massé,[3] its chief executive and mathematician.

The Fourth French Plan is more, however, than a signal example of prospective planning. It is, in its construction, a process of concerted economy realized through the co-operation of the various economic actors: *entrepreneurs*, workers, administrators. Instead of responding to a situation of conflict with

---

[1] Gaston Berger: *Phenomenologie du Temps et Prospective* (PUF, Paris, 1964).
[2] François Perroux: *L'Economie du XXe Siecle* (PUF, Paris, 1961); *Le IVe Plan Français* (PUF, Paris, 1962).
[3] Pierre Massé: *Le Choix des Investissements* (Dunod, Paris, 1959).

defensive attitudes, such co-operation produces a dynamic development which each year offers the rewards of a larger surplus. How and to what extent is this possible without stumbling into inflation? Why is it that the *Fifth* French Plan, which will be an improvement on the Fourth, could provide a model for the National Economic Development Council in Britain? How far is it regionalized and how far must it be so? These are the problems which these chapters set out to answer.

¶Practical consideration of the national aspect of the Fourth French Plan can be undertaken in three steps: (1) Who is doing the planning?; (2) How effective is it?; (3) How democratic is it?

THE PROGRAMMERS AND THE DECISION

¶Some brief acquaintance with the setting, the participants, and the substance of the Plan will help to answer the question of the identity of the planners. The French Plan has its substance in the so-called Modernization Commissions (*Commissions de Modernisation*). There is much diversity between these many groups, due to the nature of the activity and concentration of each branch, to the importance of public enterprise in that specific sector, to the role of public finance, and even to the date when the commission was created. These things affect the composition of the commissions as well as their work.

Modernization commissions

¶The participants in the Modernization Commissions have steadily grown in numbers. The first four-year plan had eight commissions and 494 members. The fourth four-year plan had twenty-six commissions and 1,006 members, including 114 trade unionists mainly of the *Confederation française des travailleurs chrétiens*. The *Commissariat au plan*, itself, is a public relations agency, which has no more than forty-six members. The *Institut national de statistique et d'etudes economiques* (INSEE) and the *Service des etudes economiques et financieres du Ministere des Finances* (SEEF)[4] provide the basic statistics, draw up the model, and establish the social accounting for the programme. All this work is done under the direction of M.Claude Gruson, polytechnician and inspector of finance, who is, with Pierre Massé, the body and soul of French planning doctrine.

4 These two public services have recently been merged.

And, as we said, in the various Commissions high civil servants of the different ministries draw up the official reports. All in all, 202 civil servants have worked in the Commissions of the Fourth Plan.

The commissions delegate particular responsibilities to work teams which vary in strength from three to one hundred members and include trade unionists, mostly *Confederation française des travailleurs chrétiens*.[5] The commission work-teams never vote on an agenda but, through discussion, attempt to find points of agreement. The reports of the teams and of the commissions are generally drawn up by civil servants.

The work of the commissions is defined in a government document of June 1960. They have 'to determine particular objectives and the ways and means to accomplish them in order that they may co-ordinate them in a coherent manner in the synthetic work of the plan'. The work of the Chemical Commission provides a good example: (1) it works out in detail the chemical goals by product and by region; (2) if necessary, it makes changes to the general objective of the first draft of the plan, both for its own branch and for other connected branches; (3) it states precisely the conditions necessary for realization of particular objectives. Commissions, of course, do not take decisions, but propose and give advice for all the problems of the sector. The agricultural commission, for example, has very considerably enlarged the scope of the problems that it had been asked to study. These problems, in fact, differ from commission to commission. In the industrial commissions, they are mainly questions of projection in actual figures of current production and little is asked about problems of investment, except in the case of the chemical industry. On the other hand, in the commissions dealing with programmes of public investment, such as the universities, the health services, transportation, and communication, even agriculture, the stress is put on collective equipment.

[5] The CFTC altered its name to CFDT in 1965.

commission	total	unions	agri-culture	entre-preneurs	profes-sional syndi-cates	civil servants	others
Agriculture	66	4	15	3	20	9	15
Artisanal	28	4		9	10	2	3
Batiment et travaux publics	43	8		8	13	6	8
Carburants	33	4		18	3	3	5
Chimie	41	4	1	23	5	4	4
Commerce	39	4		6	18	3	8
D.O.M.	39	4		3	3	14	15
Financement	46	4		15	5	20	2
Energie	42	8		9	3	11	11
Equipement culturel	59	4		3	4	12	36
Equipement sanitaire et social	39	4		1	8	10	16
Equipement scolaire	27	4	1	2	4	11	5
Equipement urbain	48	4		1	3	18	22
Habitation	30	4		2	4	5	15
Industries agricoles	70	4	2	15	38	8	3
Industries de Transformation	68	8		19	32	7	2
Main-d'œuvre	31	4		2	7	9	9
Mines et Melaux non ferreux	23	4		9	3	5	2
Peches maritimes	29	2		7	9	7	4
P. et T.	17	4		1	3	8	1
Radiotelevision	17	4		1	4	8	1
Tourisme	33	4		4	14	2	9
Siderurgie	51	4		23	18	1	5
Transports	87	12	1	15	8	19	32
OTAL GENERAL	1,006	114	20	198	239	202	233

urce: Report by Maurice Halff on 'Methods of Elaboration of the Fifth Plan' before
Conseil economique et social I O, 7/12/63.

BLE 1 Members of the Fourth Plan commissions by categories

Administrative procedure ¶ The substance of the Plan is more an indication of the objectives than a blue-print of how these objectives are to be attained. Indeed, only the heading of the Plan is a decision at all. The details of the programme are a simple orientation. The Fourth Economic Plan is a Law of very special character. It comprised only four general articles providing the general orientation of the annexed report which, just as a treaty, is not discussed or voted article by article. This very short text, only, has the authority of law.

What is the administrative procedure which gives birth to this Law? First, a decree in the *Conseil d'Etat* prescribes the preparation of the Plan. Second, a simple decree states the nomination of members of the *Commissions de Modernisation*. And third, the text of the plan and the annexed report is submitted to the *Conseil Economique et Social* for advice and to the Council of Ministers. Fourth, a bill is submitted to Parliament. Fifth, an annual control or review of the plan exists through the Budget. The Law of August 4, 1962, approving the Fourth French Plan, stated that, for the Fifth, a preliminary approval of general objectives by Parliament will be necessary.[6] The rate of growth, the proportion of investment and consumption, the structure of final consumption, and the general orientation of social and regional policy will be fixed by general deliberation and debate. Thus the plan will come before Parliament: first, to fix the general goals and, second, to approve the definitive version of the text. The first decision will most probably be taken in the light of a few alternative models which sketch the consequences of three or four sets of goals.[7]

What is generally called *The Plan* is simply an annexed report and is purely a statement of intentions. It gives general directions about the determination of such particular objectives as production, consumption or manpower, or about public and private investment. It puts no obligation whatsoever even upon the government. As for the private sector of the economy, such obligations could appear only through special measures known

[6] This was done in November 1964.
[7] Cf. The Report by Maurice Halff: *Methodes d'Elaboration du Ve Plan* (presented before the Conseil Economique et Social, JO, 7th December 1963).

as '*quasi contrats*'. For example, finance for new investment is granted *if* the firm agrees to retain its existing labour force until it can be switched to the new activity. Under 'industrial establishment contracts', firms complying with State directives can also enjoy vocational training centres adapted to their requirements, recreational provision for their staff, and modern industrial and commercial facilities. None of these requirements, however, has any legal force, not even the *quasi contrat* which is often signed on the one part by a great number of ministries and on the other by a syndicate of *entrepreneurs*. The stipulations are no more than a moral pledge but, in fact, they are effective. To what extent it is the same for the entire French economy we shall now examine.

HOW EFFECTIVE IS FRENCH PLANNING?

¶It is very difficult to measure the results of a Plan accurately, especially when it is no more than a statement of intention or of direction. Such measurement has to be approached in two steps. We shall outline first the role of the different tools and, second, we shall try to measure their combined effect upon the French economy. The main tools of the French plan are (*a*) investment in public services; (*b*) financial incentives to private industry; and (*c*) the general prospective scheme as a guide to national objectives.

General considerations

The efficiency of the plan rests firmly on investment and mainly on that sector financed directly or indirectly by the State. To gauge the volume of investment in public services, it is necessary to add local government budgets and investment in nationalized enterprises to central government capital budgeting, and to deduct the financing of private activity. In 1960 this investment in the public sector amounted to 40 per cent of total gross investment. It slightly declined during 1963. Nevertheless, public investment has, in fact, been the determining factor in both the first and fourth economic plans. The first was concerned with such basic sectors as coal, steel, and transportation, the fourth with collective investment. Collective investment is the result of the large post-war increase in the birth rate and of the spontaneous aspiration of all progressive peoples to greater

knowledge, better health, increased consumption, and reduction in hours of work. Collective consumption takes the form of
hospital building programmes; youth centres; city and motor-
way development; telecommunications; development of green
belts, tourist centres, and the like. This collective consumption
was largely integrated in the fourth plan but the democratic push
of the fifth plan will create new priority choices between the
demands of individual consumption and consumption financed
through the Budget.

Of course, there is no legal obligation towards this investment
in the public sector. Nevertheless, public sector investment has
a polarization effect and creates inducements and incentives in
associated sectors. For example, the electronics industry sells
80 per cent of its output to the public administration. An
innovation in the technique of telephony, linking it with electronic computers, would have as great an impact as the development of atomic industries. Heavy electrical apparatus and
equipment is also largely linked to public investment. The same
is true for housing. But this brings us to study the financial
incentives to private industry.[8]

The plan comprises a system of financial incentives to private
activity. The tools are many. The principal ones concern the
basic sectors of steel and aluminium production where price
control plus public financing amounts to a control of investment. Here, the plan is largely a programme for the steel and
aluminium industries. Other incentives, whether general or
regional, are purely financial. Amongst the general ones we find
(*a*) credit control through the *Credit National*. All medium-term
credit over 2·5 million francs is handed over for approval to the
Commissariat au Plan; (*b*) control by the Ministry of Finance
of every private bond issue over 1 million francs and on all
increase in capital aimed at tax exemption; (*c*) control through
selective tax exemption of the tax on value added and on
amortization.

Special incentives   ¶ Special regional incentives also exist: loans, grants (which were
increased in 1964), and rate reductions (which are disappear-

---

[8] Housing raises the problem of the ratio of cost to be covered by
budgeting or by the rent occupier.

ing). However, we will return to regional planning later. A word must be said at this point about contractual dealing (*quasi contrats*). In 1957 one such contract was signed with the car industry which committed itself to export two-thirds of its increased production. Another signed with the *Forges et Acieries de la Loire* postponed the decision to cease the activities of its *Boucau* establishment. Let me repeat, however, that there is no legal status for such *sui generis* agreements.

However, the numerous tools that we have described are not always as properly co-ordinated as they ought to be. To begin with, co-ordination, in most cases, is not the responsibility of the Administration of the plan, which appears once more as a public relations agency. It is the *Fonds de Developpement Economique et Social* (FDES) which does the job under the leadership of M. Bloch Lainé, and in some special cases sends its decision for approval to the Commissariat. In other cases, the job is done by the Ministry of Finance with approval, in certain cases, of the Commissariat. Many specialized forms of subsidy, in particular regional ones, are left without proper co-ordination. It is also of interest to note that grant incitation is most helpful for the small and medium-size enterprises. In their case, also, the lack of initiative and technical skill may be remedied by the dynamism of two research corporations specially created to advise them in conversion and decentralization or, better, delocalization; the SODIC[9] and the SOFICEMA.

From a more general viewpoint, prospective planning helps private industry in the sense that it reduces economic uncertainty as far as the future is concerned. It provides a brake on over-investment and cartelization. It provides systematic economic information. In market research it substitutes clear and farsighted interconnections for the obscurity of short-sighted studies of small fragments of the market. It creates *coherence*.

¶ To what extent has this planned economy increased the rate of French economic growth and improved the economic structure of the country?

Increase in annual growth

It is useful to compare the different rates of growth and capital

[9] Societé pour la conversion et le developpement industriel.

coefficients of different western economies during the decade 1950–1960. French planning, after all, began in 1946, and can be divided into three periods. First comes the 'Jean Monnet' period from 1945 to 1951 when the CECA was created. In 1951 also, there was created in France the SEEF to collate the national accounts. The second period is the 'Etienne Hirsch' of the second and third plans. It begins in 1951 and ends in 1958, the year when the Treaty of Rome became operational. Third is the 'Pierre Massé', period from 1959 on; the period of the fourth and fifth plans. Thus what is under consideration, so far as France is concerned, is not so much the improved method of the later years as the effects of the earlier planning. At all events, the results are of great interest if we recall the military and political difficulties of France during the fifties.[10]

To what extent then has the annual rate of growth of the French economy, compared to that of foreign countries, increased through the action, in each industrial sector, of the vertical commissions in eliminating superfluous investment; and of the horizontal commissions of manpower and finance, in securing general economic coherence? The following table may provide the answer.

TABLE 2
Annual rate of
growth 1954–1962

country	employment	productivity	GNP
United Kingdom	0·56	1·87	2·43
Sweden	1·12	2·81	3·93
France	0·15	4·80	4·95
Italy	1·82	4·41	6·23
Germany	1·92	4·57	6·49

Source: OCDE, and T. P. Hill, *Economic Journal*, June 1964.

It is apparent that the French economy has grown faster than that of Great Britain and even of Sweden but less rapidly than that of Italy and Germany. The superiority of the last-named two countries, however, may be accounted for, to a large extent, by population pressure and reduction of unemployment. If, for example, we consider Germany, we find the following figures.

[10] On these aspects of French planning read Jean Fourastié: *La Planification Economique en France* (PUF, 1963).

	1950-60	1961	1962	1963	1964	1961-64
Germany	7·5	5·6	4·4	3·0	4·5	4·4

TABLE 3
Rate of growth of
GNP constant
prices

Source: Bericht über die Wirtschatfsenwicklung im Jahre 1963.

With the end of underemployment in Germany, it would appear that the rate of growth has been reduced to something below the French rate of 5·5 per cent, which proved so difficult, in 1964, to reduce to 5 per cent in order to curb a moderate inflationary pressure.

However, there is another aspect less favourable to France. The French rate of economic growth seems to have been more costly than that of other countries, if we consider investment. In Europe, growth rates have been strongly associated with the share of national product devoted to fixed investment[11] as shown in the following table:

TABLE 4
Gross fixed
investment and
capital coefficients
in Europe
1954-1962

	gross investment share in GNP		rate of growth of GNP		capital coefficient	
	(1) total	(2) machinery and equipment	(3) total	(4) per person employed	(5) (1)/(3)	(6) (2)/(4)
Germany	22·5	11·6	6·49	4·50	3·47	2·58
Italy	20·8	9·0	6·23	4·33	3·35	2·07
France	18·3	8·3	4·95	4·74	3·60	1·75
US	16·6	5·7	3·39	2·17	4·88	2·67
UK	15·2	7·8	2·43	1·87	6·33	4·10

In France then, for a rate of increase of 1 per cent the capital coefficient is 3·6, showing a smaller efficiency of capital than in Germany, where the rate is 3·47, but a much larger one than in the United States and in England where the rates are 4·88 and 6·33.

[11] See T. P. Hill: *Growth and Investment According to International Comparisons* (Economic Journal, June 1964). The coefficient of correlation is 0.96 between growth rate and investment shares for the United States and the four largest European countries, accounting together for seven-eighths of the total output of Western Europe and North America.

K

Moreover, if we recognize that a large part of German and Italian growth has been the result of substantial increases in employment, which have been lacking in France up to 1962, we must admit that the French performance is remarkable. A significant way to show this is to compute the rate of growth of GNP per person employed and to compare it to investment. The coefficients become 3·89 for France, 4·89 for Italy, 5·00 for Germany. Thus for the same rate of increase of 1 per cent of GNP per person employed, France has had to invest less than Italy and Germany, and the productivity of French capital appears to be the largest. There are two explanations of this; the first is the part played by productive investment (machinery and equipment) in the total investment of each country and, from this point of view, the results are even more in favour of France where the capital coefficient is 1·75, as shown on Table 4. The second reason would be technical progress and a better functioning of the whole economy, namely the influence of the Plan.

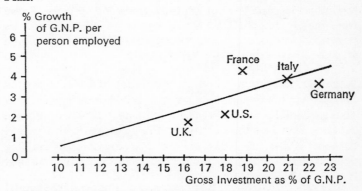

(This reasoning can only be valid between countries with comparable growth rates. Indeed, as T. P. Hill shows, the relation between investment and GNP is not proportional but commonly linear. The correlation equation is $g = -\cdot357 + 0\cdot38\,i$ where g is the growth of output per person and i total gross investment. This relation implies that the ratio of gross investment to growth declines sharply as investment increases. It is the marginal coefficient and not the mean coefficient which is constant as shown on the graph. The equation of the re-gression line implies that an extra 2.63 % $\left(\dfrac{1}{0.38}\right)$ of GNP has to be invested to secure an extra 1% growth. But even on this safer basis, the performance of France is far above the mean, represented by the regression line.)

In order to ascertain the influence of the Plan on the structure of the French economy, we must try to discover to what extent the Plan is responsible for a change in allocation and employment of resources, both in terms of the composition of the national product and of the distribution of national income.

Some basic 'tough' sectors respond promptly to planning control. These are the heavy industries, the nationalized indus-tries (energy and communications), and the socio-cultural sec-tor, construction and urban development, heavy electrical, electronic, and nuclear industries. Some 'smooth' sectors follow at a distance: agriculture, food manufacturing industries, and, more generally, the agricultural complex, common manufactur-ing industries, and last but not least, trade and services. These were mainly responsible for the economy lagging behind its targets.[12] Hence some political movements and the importance ascribed to services in the Fourth plan.

¶Another important point is international trade. François Perroux[13] in his illuminating study of the Fourth French Plan casts a clear light on this problem. Maurice Halff does the same in connection with the Fifth Plan. The structure of the French economy is evolving rapidly. From 1958 onwards the country opened itself increasingly to foreign markets and foreign goods but chiefly, of course, to the other five countries of the EEC.

The Plan and foreign trade

_ Imports or exports, however, did not in France (1962) amount to more than 10 per cent of gross national product, compared to 33 per cent in Belgium, 15 per cent in Germany and in the Uni-ted Kingdom. It is nevertheless more difficult each year to gear imports through a policy of total domestic demand and the promotion of exports becomes more and more stochastic with

[12] Index 126; seven points under the target 133. Agriculture was on target 120.
[13] François Perroux: *Le IVe Plan Français* (PUF, Que sais-je, 1962).

the disappearance of traditional markets and the opening of new ones. Hence the necessity, from the French point of view, of a European economic plan.

TABLE 5
Evolution of French
foreign trade in
percentage of
ports and exports

	1958	1959	1960	1961	1962
imports from EEC	21·9	26·8	29·4	31·5	33·6
imports from AELE					11·1
imports from USA					10·3
exports to EEC	22·2	27·2	29·8	33·5	36·8
exports to AELE					16·0
exports to USA					5·8

Source: *Office statistique des communautes europiennes.*

Structural changes linked to the plan also bear upon the distribution of national income. An incomes policy has long been a tacit assumption of every plan and is linked with a policy on prices and consumption. But a precise incomes policy, understood as the determination of value added and not of fiscal redistribution, is mentioned for the first time in the Fourth Plan. In 1962, wages were over 60 per cent of national income at factor cost and agriculture accounted for less than 10 per cent of GNP at market price.

After the experience of two special committees, and reports in 1963 and 1964, a new, most interesting innovation is being introduced in the Fifth Plan. A programme in monetary values will complete the programme in real terms through the utilization of evolving prices and incomes, compatible with the realization of economic, political, and social objectives of the plan. A programme in monetary values is the frame necessary to introduce an incomes policy which aims at realizing greater justice in the standing of the different social groups.[14] The Plan

[14] 'Projet de Loi portant approbation d'un rapport sur les principales options qui commandent la preparation du cinquième Plan, 5 Novembre 1964.'

has not hitherto indicated the normal growth rate of wages, profits, agricultural incomes, and prices except in theoretical and schematical annexes. This innovation conceals some great difficulties. The main reason for this is that free collective bargaining is the law of the land, and is even incorporated in the constitution. But the Plan is indicative and will deal with broad categories. It is to some extent a treaty on incomes. Another reason is the absence of adequate statistical data except on salaries, although a great effort is being made to ascertain other sources of income. The last reason is that a complete incomes policy is impossible without a direct price policy. It is important to understand that private incomes will not any longer be determined by market forces only. As in agriculture, other social considerations will officially be introduced in the determination of value added by the factors of production.

If the Fourth development plan did not explicitly include an incomes or, better, an added value policy, it had necessarily a private and collective consumption policy. It is now well known, through Galbraith's stimulating works, that in affluent societies of America and Europe the market is governed not by the consumers but by the producers; the means which the Plan commands to deal with that problem is the momentum which it gives to collective investment. During the period of the Fourth Plan, the increase on the 1961 basis was about 50 per cent for social investment, 28 per cent for economic investment, and 23 per cent only for national consumption. France will have more hospitals, more schools, and more new towns. But there remains a final question to be answered.

HOW DEMOCRATIC IS FRENCH PLANNING?

¶In the past the plan has been controlled and enacted by the traditional techniques of democracy; in effect, by means of the annual Budget. The Fourth French Plan (1962-1965) was the first to require approval, at its inception, and as an invididual economic measure, by vote of Parliament, after consultation with the *Conseil Economique et Social*. Furthermore, the terms of approval of August 4, 1962, state that, in future, Parliament will be required to approve the main goals of the Plan, in

Parliament and the Plan

principle, before voting at a later stage on the full detailed proposals. This has been realized through the law approving a report on the main options of the Fifth Plan (1966-1970). Will this lead to a new and more democratic way of planning? Or will the Plan become, in effect, a new kind of bureaucratic process, with traditional budgetary control to give it precise legal existence, power of action, and modification? What effect will the new technical model of the Plan have on the structure of French and western democracy?

At first the Plan made no impact on legal and executive procedures, and the legal administrative hierarchy was unaffected by it. Legal authorization of the Plan was so unspecific that, to begin with, it produced no increase in the powers of bureaucracy, either in the Commissariat or in the traditional Ministry. The Law, as voted by Parliament, most closely resembles a treaty between the government and the national economy! The treaty itself is the report annexed to the three or four general articles. But this treaty is not imperative. It implies no legal or administrative obligations. There is no special sanction, and no formal control by the Judiciary, on the actions of the Administration, taken in accordance with the Economic Development Plan.[15] The Administration is required only to conform to established administrative procedure.

The enforcement of the Plan rests, *de facto*, on the stability of government and administrative action on the one hand, and on the other on the acceptance of the Plan by the nation at large; in particular, it works through the concerted interaction of the *Commissions de Modernisation* and the social groups throughout the land. Hence the importance of the 1,006 members of the *Commissions* in the Fourth Plan, and of the 114 Union representatives. Of equal importance is the power of the CES in regard to the choice of objectives (1962-1965), and its stimulating reports on the problems of execution of the Fourth Plan and the methods of elaboration of the Fifth Plan.[16] Unhappily, television inter-

---

[15] In another field the Conseil d'Etat has stated that the European Justice Court has to interpret, itself, the administrative decisions taken in accordance with the Rome Treaty.
[16] Maurice Halff: JO *Rapports du Conseil Economique et Social* (11th June, 1963, and 7th December, 1963).

views have shown that neither the layman nor the average inter-
viewer himself have any clear conception of what the Plan is all
about,[17] and the CES is not yet sufficiently integrated with and
involved in the process of democratic choice. There are signs,
however, that four successive four-year plans are having an indirect effect on the structure and customs of French political
life.

For one thing, Parliament is not adapted to elaborate and
follow out the execution of the Plan. The Assembly is heavily
enough burdened as it is with budgetary control of the resources
and expenditure of the government. Since the Second Plan, it
is true, there has been presented to Parliament an Annual Report on the measures, results, difficulties, and eventual modifications to the Plan. But this is intended mainly to shed more light
on the financial decision of the Budget and integrate the Plan
with the general economic policy of the nation. Modifications to
the Plan have in fact been the work of the Administration. The
intermediary plan which modified the Third Plan was submitted
neither to Parliament nor to the CES.

So far as the Plan is concerned, the role of Parliament is to
decide on objectives in the light of the technical advice received
from the CES. In view of its economic complexity, execution and
control of the instruments must be the responsibility of the CES.
The need for this control, its modalities and limits has been
studied in detail by the Council itself. One of the Council's main
roles is to supervise the necessary articulation of the Plan and
national Budget; national accounts and the costs of the Plan
itself. On these matters members of Parliament are powerless
vis-à-vis the economic technicians of the Administration. The
aim of such control is to determine what actions and responses
are necessary, in order to steer the economy in the direction of
the Plan's objective. Revisions to the Plan should, for easily
understandable technical reasons, be submitted to the Council.
If the choice of *objectives* rests with Parliament, the *control* of
economic execution should be the task of the Council (CES).
The *structure and process* of the Plan is in the realm of the

[17] See Pierre Bauchet: *La Planification Française* (Editions du Seuil,
1962).

concerted deliberation of the *Commissions de Modernisation* in the Commissariat. At this level the Plan is not a *contrat social* but a moral pledge.

The following scheme may clarify the position.

1 parliament	2 Modernization Commissions	3 Economic and Social Council
determination of objectives	structure and process of plan	advice on objectives economic study of the current working of the plan

The role of the Council is therefore linked with the evolution of French planning.

Effect of the Plan on French bureaucracy

¶ So far, the *central bureaucratic structure* of the Plan has not resulted in any major innovations. But, at regional level, Decrees of March 14, 1964, have brought about a decentralization reform. The Decrees create, first, a Regional Prefect (*Préfet de Région*); second, a regional administrative body; third, a Regional Economic Development Commission (*Commission de developement économique régionale*). These reforms are expressly linked, in the report leading to the Decrees, with the economic necessities of the Plan. The reforms, in fact, are regarded as a test, by the Government, of (1) the popularity of the idea of concerted planning, including the possibilities of interesting small and medium-sized enterprises (as well as the Unions) in this kind of participation in national development; and (2) of the chances of success of other reforms at *national* level, as far as the CES is concerned.

Of course, the *Commissariat au Plan* is a more powerful organization than either the German Planning Bureau or the American Council of Economic Advisers. But the *Commissariat* is not entrusted with the co-ordination of French financial and economic policy. Its role is more that of public relations, reconciling, not co-ordinating, policy. The Ministry of Finance still in many regards retains its primacy, and every inflationary pressure works in favour of the traditional, annual administrative procedure.

Nevertheless, four periods of concerted planning have left their mark on the structure of French administrative procedures. A new type of meeting – concerned with discussion and co-operation – has developed in the Modernization Commissions of the *Commissariat*. Parliamentary assemblies are characterized by open confrontation in debate, linked with maximum publicity. Publicity is an essential characteristic of the legal process. The debates of the Commission are 'restricted', as determined by economic and social imperatives. Far from being confrontations of opposed viewpoints, they are attempts at common participation, starting from points of agreement, and with the intention of arriving at general agreement without any attendant publicity save the General Report. Where the actual public execution of the Plan is concerned, there are no administrative orders but merely circulars and directives, which provide general advice for the administrators. Equally, in the private sector, the creation of *quasi* contracts between ministers on the one hand and an economic body or private industry on the other is characterized by the absence of obligations and sanctions. The *do ut des* is enough. It works. How it does so is a matter for sociologists to answer. Whether it will last and become traditional remains to be seen.

The French Plan is the best rationalization of the capitalist system yet arrived at. It is not so much a revolution as an evolution: an attempt to regulate the market system. To make it complete, it requires a coherent regional policy and an effective incomes policy. Both are slowly being created despite the delay imparted by a temporary inflationary pressure. The Fifth French Plan will be the next important step on this new and democratic road.

French Regional Planning

Involving the
nation

¶Regional planning is neither an abstract theoretical concept dreamt up by technocrats nor the camouflaged instrument of central and administrative hegemony over regional autonomy. It is the consequent response to the enlargement of local markets through the road transport revolution. It is also the straightest if hardest way to secure the participation of the entire nation in a concerted economy and a collective economic decision. It marches under the popular banners of *Paris et le desert français*[1] and *L'aménagement du territoire*.[2] These refer to two conflicting philosophies and signalize two successive and progressive points of view from which France looks to its regions.[3]

Throughout the course of the Second, Third, and Fourth Plans, regional planning slowly developed, but it is only in the current Fifth Plan (January 1966–December 1970), that it will come into full play at two different levels. In its medium-term (four years) aspect, it appears as a regionalization of the national plan to which it gives geographic precision and local adhesion; in the long-term (twenty years) aspect, it is the expression of the remodelling of the national territory (*aménagement*) and it serves

[1] By Jean François Gravier (1947), member of the Conseil Economique et Social.
[2] By Philippe Lamour (1962), President of the Commission d'Aménagement du Territoire.
[3] From 'saupoudrage' to growth points.

as a guide to national planning. There is both difficulty and paradox in a scheme which is at once a medium-term complement and a long-term guide.

MEDIUM TERM REGIONALIZATION

¶A rapid sketch of the birth of the present regional institutions may be helpful as the preliminary to the study of their actual and future functioning. From the *administrative* viewpoint, the birth of regionalization in France was the Decree of June 30, 1955, organizing the elaboration of regional programming with a view to completing the plan of modernization and capital re-equipment. This took place in the second year of the Second Plan (1954-1957). In November 1956, the borders of the present twenty-one areas of regional activities were defined. But spontaneous action grew only very slowly and in a disordered way. There were few regional programmes and fewer genuine ones among them. These were in essence little more than catalogues of resources and needs with few quantitative evaluations and no distinction between objective, structure and means. A basic reason for this was that the different administrations waited until November 1956 before harmonizing their technical geographical boundaries[4] to the new regional ones; and until 1959 before establishing an inter-departmental conference (*conférence interdépartementale*) between the civil servants. In the private sector, the *Comités d'Aménagement* were mostly at *départemental* level. It was only in 1961 that the 'Regional Expansion Committees', a genuinely regional consultative body, were given official sanction. Nevertheless, an empirical regional framework slowly took shape. It showed a lack of homogeneity and administrative command. Hence the regional administrative reform of March 1964, known as the 'deconcentration administrative'.

Today the twenty-one *circonscriptions d'action régionale* are headed by a Regional Prefect responsible for the execution of the Plan and for programmes of special regional concern. He

Regional organization

[4] The ministerial decision from November 28, 1956, establishes the programming regions; the Decree from June 2, 1960, organizes administrative harmonization within the regions.

has authority to make decisions, in certain cases, without referring the issue to Paris. The Regional Prefect is or will be served
by a specialized staff, termed 'mission'. He will be assisted by
two consultative bodies: (1) the regional administrative conference comprises all the senior civil servants, the prefects, the
regional treasurer, the inspector-general of the economy and
representatives of the different ministries; (2) the Regional
Commission for Economic Development replaces and enlarges
the original Regional Expansion Committees. These still survive as research and public relations bodies. This new regional
commission will have from twenty to fifty members, a quarter
of them being local councillors, another quarter nominated by
the Prime Minister. The remainder will represent employers'
organizations, chambers of commerce, and trade unions. The
Commission is established for a period of five years. It is
required to give advice on the economic and social development
of the region as well as on its remodelling. Thus the administrative reform of March 1964 appears as a test of the willingness
of the country to participate in the Plan and of its keenness for
economic planning in general.

Financial   From the fiscal point of view, the French effort to create
structure   financial institutions has been less ambitious. The Decree of
June 30, 1955, created Regional Development Societies (SDR),
which are regional investment trusts combined with some banking activity. They were created with the participation of the
great national banks and the local savings associations. In order
that their market studies may be broad, the SDR do not limit
their sphere of action to one official programming region where
this is not important or extensive enough. Fifteen SDR in fact
cover the whole country with the exception of Paris. Most of
them have a capital of 7·5 million francs. Their actions are coordinated through the *Crédit National* which has a seat on each
administrative board, with a participation of 5 per cent. At the
end of 1962 the total operations amounted to 756 million francs.

Next, *Sociétés d'Equipement* are semi-public organizations
created with the help of the *Caisse des Dépots et Consignation*.
Their aim is to build the necessary basic infrastructure for
industrial zones, zones of agricultural betterment, and zones of

urban growth. Their work is co-ordinated by the *Société Centrale pour l'Equipement du Territoire* (SCET).

To these one must, of course, add the activity of the *Fond de Dévelopement Economique et Social* (FDES). Created in 1959, it is a 'special account' of the Treasury acting as a regional 'Fabrizi banker'[5] through its Committee 1 ter; between 1955 and 1962 it distributed 240 million francs by way of 'special equipment grants (bonuses)' and 220 million francs of long-term loans. Bonuses are now the main method of government assistance.[6]

This brings us to the point where we must study the present and future functioning of regionalization. The regionalization of the plan is based on two types of economic instruments: (1) financial incentives to private regional localization throughout the national territory; and (2) the co-ordination in each programming region of investment, for the most part public but tentatively private. We will take the second point first.

¶Regional co-ordination of investment has been practised for the first time during the Fourth Plan, under the cryptic title of *Tranches Opératoires* (operational slices of the Plan). These, in fact, are *annual slices* of public investment to be allocated to and appropriated by each region. They link the regional plans to the national plan and form part of four-year slices worked out, on the evidence submitted by each region, by the Commissariat's committee of regional planning. The preparation of this regional capital budget is made by the Regional administrative conference. The administrative reform of March 1964 gives to each regional Prefect all the power necessary to determine the regional slice of the national plan, in collaboration with the Conference. The reform decrees that each regional Prefect will submit a yearly report to the Prime Minister.

Public investment

There exist, in fact, three types of public investment in each region. So far as national public investment is concerned, the Prefect is informed and is empowered to make observations. Where regional public investment is concerned, the Prefect distributes the whole amount of the various delegated credits

[5] A banker making grants. One could also speak of a Marshall banker.
[6] One must add the action of the FIAT, a special fund of 150 million francs at the disposition of the Prime Minister acting through the *Délégation à l'Aménagement du Territoire*.

within the limits set by the plan. Indeed, the power of decision which formerly belonged to the senior regional civil servants in each branch is transferred to the Prefect. Finally, where *départe-mental* public investment is concerned, the Prefect advises the minister how the allocation of the specific appropriation should be made. So much for the executive side of regional investment planning. On the *quasi*-legislative side, the Economic Development Commission, which is only a consultative body, offers advice on the regional aspects of the national plan and on the *regional slice* of national investment. This might seem to be a means of integrating private investment planning with public equipment, as the *Conseil Economique et Social* (CES) has so often advised.[7] But all this is largely for the Fifth Plan to execute in detail. The Fourth Plan is essentially, in this regard, a piece of regional training and *mise au point*.

Indeed, the report on the general orientation of the Fifth Plan describes regionalization in three phases. The first is included in the orientation report itself, by the *Commission Nationale d'Aménagement du Territoire*, but on a long-term basis. The second phase, after approval of the orientation report, is the work, on a medium term basis, of the commissions of regional economic development of the Commissariat. The third phase, after the approval of the plan by Parliament, is the 'operational slices' procedure which has just been described.

The financial incentives to private regional localization have, similarly, been entirely reorganized in 1964. They have been placed under the co-ordination of the *Délégation à l'Aménage-ment du Territoire*, headed by Olivier Guichard, which was established in February 1963. Its policy was decreed in an appendix to the Finance Act 1964, headed 'Regionalization of the capital budget for 1964 and co-ordination of public invest-ment so far as the remodelling of the territory is concerned'. This long-term aspect will be studied in the next paragraph. Here we concentrate on the reform of financial aids which, like the administrative reform, has been the work of the Delegation. The oldest tool used by the central authorities to execute their

---

[7] Cf. *Methodes d'Elaboration du Ve Plan* (JO Conseil Economique et Social, 7th December 1963).

regional policies was neither negligible nor adequate. It consisted largely of fiscal advantages for land and building development, in low-interest loans, and primarily in subsidies which took the form of grants of up to 20 per cent of total investment, with a maximum of 11,000 francs for each newly created job; or in the offer of a free site for a factory. A large number of municipalities sell factory buildings on a rent-sale basis, payable over fifteen to twenty years with an annual interest rate of 6·5 per cent. Before the reform, some fifteen hundred factories had been established each year in the French provinces, creating about 20,000 new jobs. It is hoped that, as a consequence of this reform, some 50,000 new jobs per year will be created. For purposes of comparison, let us remember that the growth of the Paris area (PADOG) creates 40,000 new jobs each year. Moreover, nearly half of all the new factories are being set up within two hundred kilometres of the capital. The rate of growth and the localization of new industries in the metropolitan area was partly the result of the highly complex system of financial aid and of the cumbersomeness of the administrative procedure. No one was absolutely certain of receiving assistance. The reform, therefore, has two aims: clarity and automatic action. The industrialist must know with certainty where the government wants him to go, and what advantages he will obtain by going there.

France is divided into five zones. The first, called *quasi-automatic*, is West France. It goes from the Channel south to the Midi Pyrennees region and east as far as Ardêche in the Rhône-Alpes region. Within zone 1 most favourable treatment is given to eight foci: Cherbourg, Brest, Lorient, Nantes, La Rochelle, Limoges, Bordeaux, and Toulouse. Here the grant will be of the order of 20 per cent of the total investment for the establishment of a new factory, and 10 per cent for its extension as compared with 10 per cent and 5 per cent for the rest of the zone. The second zone is the 'conversion' zone, and it receives an industrial adaptation grant of up to 20 per cent of the operative costs. It is, to a large part, formed of the mining and textile districts. The third zone is a set of slow-growing towns in the rich part of France. This zone can receive only certain fiscal

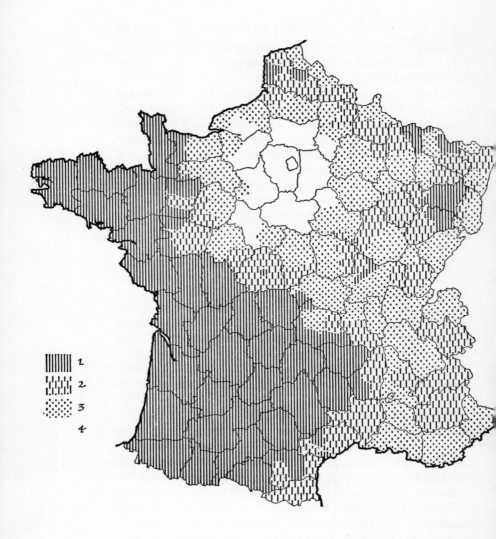

MAP 7
OPERATIONAL ZONES OF FINANCIAL AID
1 : Large aid 2 : Medium sized aid 3 : Small aid 4 : nil

advantages. Of course, the first two zones may also take advantage of reduced taxation. The fourth zone forms the rich part of France, the Paris region excluded. Here there is no automaticity whatsoever. Decentralization operations will be studied individually, on their merits, in order to benefit from detaxation. The fifth zone, where no advantages can be granted, is a large region centred on Paris, which includes not only the PADOG (Seine, Seine et Oise, Seine et Marne) but l'Oise, Rouen in Seine Maritime, Evreux et les Andelys in Eure, Dreux Chartres and Châteaudun in Eure et Loir, le Loiret, Vendôme and Blois in Loir et Cher, Sens in Yonne, Château-Thierry and Soissons in Aisne. This financial region corresponds to no traditional administrative border. As you will see, its shape is determined by the demands of long-term prospective planning.

PROSPECTIVE REMODELLING

¶Prospective remodelling is a preoccupation of long-term development policy. It leads to decisions about the economic infra-structure. It affects the location of industrial and housing development; it influences the way of living and the human environment. Remodelling is determined by interconnections other than those of the medium-term models; namely on relations between urbanization and industrialization, between the role of universities and scientific research on the one hand, and regional economic progress on the other. Even when these relations are not yet quantified, knowledge of their existence and structure is necessary to understand the direction and quality of development. *Location of industry, etc.*

Prospective is no mere classical plotting of a spontaneous evolution even on a long-term basis. It is the definition and choice of a set of long-term goals, the determination of the possibility of attaining them and the specification of the possible means of their attainment. It requires proper institutions, precise definition of programming regions adapted to the objectives, and the specification of a long-term policy. We will study these three points in succession.

¶Every policy requires for its attainment an executive body and a representative adviser. In France the first of these is the *Responsibility*

L

Délégation à l'Aménagement du Territoire et à l'Action Régionale. The second is the *Commission Nationale de l'Aménagement du Territoire.* Both of these were established on February 14, 1963. Linking the two institutions is the *Délégué à l'Aménagement,* who is also Vice-President of the Commission.

The Delegation is directly responsible to the Prime Minister. It is a co-ordinating and dynamic organism for the preparation of the necessary regional decisions of the government. It studies the regional work of every French ministry, and co-ordinates these so far as investment programmes are concerned. The synthetic task of the delegation is, therefore, to prepare the groundwork for the deliberation of specialized inter-ministerial committees and to control their decisions. On the basis of long-term prospective, it deals with public works and infrastructure policy (principally urbanization), regional administrative reforms, and financial incentives.

The Commission is a new *horizontal* group within the *Commissariat Général au Plan.* Its task is to study the special characteristics of long-term economic development. Its reports and conclusions are integrated in the Plan. A good example is the fourth part of the law on the main options of the Fifth Plan. In fact, the Commission acts at two levels: (1) in advance of the work of the *vertical* commissions, in order to clarify the first choice of goals determined by Parliament; (2) during the complete elaboration of the Plan, in order to advance the horizon twenty years ahead (for the Fifth Plan up to 1985). Moreover, through its subcommissions, it will endeavour to establish operational links with the vertical commissions in order to co-ordinate regional and sectoral aspects. Of course, the vertical point of view will always be dominant. At present, the *Commission Nationale d'Aménagement* is composed of six groups. The first is concerned with general prospectives; the second, third, and fourth with the spatial remodelling of primary, secondary, and tertiary sectors; the fifth, and the most important, with the urban framework; the sixth with communications.

Types of models ¶ A long-term regional border cannot be the same as a medium-term one, for the very good reason that new variables enter into the decision model. It is less precise than the medium-term model, since economic, sociological, and demographic factors become more and more uncertain in proportion to the length of the period of time being dealt with. Time is a fourth dimension. Long-term prospective is a view of the far distance. We see a larger horizon and, therefore, can better judge how to remodel the territory, but we cannot see details with the same clarity. To achieve this we must reduce the long-term view to shorter term units. Long-term regions (twenty years) will therefore be larger than medium-term ones (five years). Here we have to relate two factors: the model itself and the human or technical possibilities of implementing it.

Where models[8] are concerned, France is currently experimenting with two types. First is a model of homogeneous regions which attempts to sketch, by large zones, on the one hand the regionalization of economic activities, and on the other the demographic evolution over the period to 1985. The second is a polarization model which begins with the urban network, its probable evolution and localization of population in 1985, and attempts to find the distribution of activities fitted to these new demographic structures. Of course, there is a confrontation of both models in order that they can correct and modify each other.

The homogeneous model suggested a division of France into three large regions each with a different evolution. The model conceived a rapidly developing zone in the south-east of France from Lyon to Marseilles, linked with the already developed zone of the east and north; an underdeveloped zone growing at a slower rate than the two other regions, in the centre, west, and south-west; and the very special region of Paris (PADOG)[9] surrounded by the Parisian basin. France is therefore studied from the viewpoint of employment and goals which emerge as hypotheses are arrived at to help the western regions. Sixty per cent of the increase in industrial job opportunities ought to be created in the west. What then will be the impact of this on the national growth rate? This appalling figure is, in fact, a skillful political

[8] Model is taken here in the sense of a class of structure.
[9] Plan d'Aménagement et d'Organisation Générale de la Région Parisienne.

gesture towards the regions as opposed to the metropolitan area.

A large part of the so-called west is in fact the large Paris region, which – in 1962 – extends much further than the PADOG (Seine, Seine et Oise, Seine et Maine) and includes l'Oise, le Loiret with Orleans, l'Eure et Loir, l'Yonne and a large part of Aisne and Eure. This has been recognized in terms of the fifth zone of financial aid. The PADOG definition of Paris is perfect where urbanism is concerned but not so good in terms of industrial development. In the larger polarized Paris area, industrial growth will be spontaneous, efficient, and easily attained. It will present no problems for the rate of national economic progress.

In the smaller western region a distinction must be made between the north (Brittany) where demography is buoyant, and the south (Bordeaux-Toulouse) where the potential surplus of active population is much less. All this becomes much clearer when we look at the polarization model.

Regional metropolises   ¶ In France, as elsewhere, there is a correlation between industrialization and urbanization. The demographic trend towards the towns will be determined by the rural exodus and the progress of agricultural productivity. In 1962 the population of France was 46 million. In 1985 it will be 60 million. Hence the importance of the nodes and the hierarchy of the French urban structure. What is the state of things today, and what can be predicted for 1985?

A most interesting report by J. Hautreux and M. Rochefort points out that the huge polarized Parisian region accounts for about half of the national territory. A north-western region has Nantes-Saint Nazaire as its metropolis. Two south-western regions are headed by Bordeaux and Toulouse. Aix-Marseilles is the centre for the Provence region; Lyon-St Etienne for the Rhône-Alpes; Nancy -Metz for Lorraine; Strasbourg for Alsace; and Lille-Roubaix-Tourcoing for the north. Each regional metropolis is surrounded by regional centres and their satellites.

Long-term regional policy is influenced by this situation, by the disproportion existing between Paris and the largest French towns; even between these and the largest foreign towns. A first objective, therefore, is to develop, or even to establish, a top

MAP 8

LONG TERM REGIONAL PLANNING

1: Regional Metropolises   2: Regional Centres   3: Regional Satellite towns   4: Towns at present possessing regional importance, which ought to be preserved

level of regional urban hierarchy. As we know, this hierarchy is created by the functions of the towns and ordered by the radius of their zones of influence. At the top, a regional metropolis or conurbation must be able to co-ordinate the principal functions necessary for the political, economic, and cultural life of some five million people. The measures necessary to achieve this must be taken within the period of the Fifth and Sixth Plans, in order to develop these poles of equilibrium.

Comparisons between France and Britain stress the absence in the former of the establishment of real New Towns. Sarcelles, Peage du Rousillon and, worse, Mourenx, do not merit this title. As Pinchemel points out, they have no social nor occupational diversification. He adds: 'the urban phenomenon is biological; it is neither physics nor geometry. Now, a cell does not grow indefinitely ... when it reaches a given size it divides and gives birth to new cells which remain linked in a diversified tissue.'[10] This would perhaps be the best solution for a regional metropolis once it has attained a population of a million inhabitants. Lyon's PADOG might become an example in this respect. But public opinion is not aware of it.

At the intermediary level, the urban hierarchy is composed of regional centres whose functions affect a group of two or three million inhabitants. For the most part, they are capitals of programming regions. The 'ground level' is composed of small towns whose influence extends to about 100,000 inhabitants.

The rapid growth of the Paris region makes it imperative to promote prompt action in favour of regional metropolitan centres. Of course, Paris (with the industrialized north, and east) is the key to French competition in the European market, and must not be discouraged; yet the regional poles of equilibrium must be favoured. In this sphere of urban economic development, State intervention is the determining factor. In its hands lie the location of administrative services, of hospitals, schools, technical colleges, and universities. To a great extent, through the operation of financial grants, it is the same with housing programmes and factory building.

We are thus confronted with models based on three homo-

[10] Pinchemel: *Urbanisation Prospective. No. II* (PUF 1964).

geneous regions and nine polarized regions.[11] Parliament has taken these as a general guide when fixing the goals for the Fifth Economic Plan.

Where human and technological potential is concerned, two points are of great importance. First, the *number* of such regions should not be made inflexible, so that the first sketch can be worked out in finer detail sector by sector. Second, the large, long-term regions should – for administrative purposes and for reasons of local consultation – include an integer of medium-term programming regions. A third and less important point is that they should not be too far distanced from the organization dealing with public financial aid. This is not exactly a logical need but one that would create less confusion in the mind of the public.

¶ Owing to the geographical conditions of production, the agricultural study must differ from the industrial approach in that it must be based on the homogeneous region. The two aspects are chiefly linked by the rural exodus. Another and more positive link is what we have called the agricultural complex.

French agriculture

The structure and fragmentation of agricultural property is a technical disadvantage which might be solved through geographical grouping of divided lots, and SAFER.[12] The need for local Technical Demonstration Centres at growth points as well as the desirability of associating the peasant with the transformation of his products argues in favour of the creation of regional agricultural centres.

In 1962, there were in France 36,000 rural municipalities, of which 17,000 had less than three hundred inhabitants in the chief village.[13] This is one of the sociological causes of under-development. Today the use of the motor vehicle in agriculture permits its regrouping in rural centres with some elementary urbanization and possessing the basic facilities of collective life, with a population of only one or two thousand. In fact, this evolution is already at work in France. Such small rural towns

[11] Eight poles of equilibrium, plus Paris.
[12] Société d'Aménagement Foncier et d'Etablissement Rural.   Loi 5 Août 1960.
[13] Cf. André Grandpierre: *Le Regroupement de l'Habitat Rural dans Urbanisation* (Prospective II, PUF 1964).

could be the development poles of the new agricultural complex. They would help to stop the great migration towards the metropolis.

It must be stressed that the rural complex should integrate all the food, leather, wood, and fibre industries linked with agricultural products. An interindustry input-output analysis has shown in the previous chapters that the development of such a complex is most helpful for an already developed country. Indeed it is through the localization of these transformation industries in rural areas that agricultural activities can be valorized. Compared to this the determination of a European price for wheat is secondary. Following the lead of Maurice Byé,[14] one could envisage specialization of the agricultural West of France, in these activities which are to a certain extent traditional but unsufficiently developed. One could envisage a change of locale of the textile industry from north and east to the south-west, and for the same reasons as in the United States, namely the wage level. These industries have of course a slower rate of growth than the new propulsive industries, but their fast migration to the south-west could regionally double the national rate and for a time (five to ten years) outgrow the most buoyant industries of the north and east. This push could revive the slow growing part of France.

*   *   *

To conclude, it is important to point out the importance of a powerful regional authority to develop, on the one hand, regional coherence, and on the other to create, through a study of the polarization of towns and villages, a harmonious hierarchy. The greatest danger is always that of the unique and 'primate' city in an empty hinterland deprived of any intermediary towns.

Let us never forget that we are building a world for men, not for the sake of producing more gadgets, more armaments and more aggressiveness. And let us remember the fundamental difference between growth, development, and progress. Growth

[14] Maurice Byé: *Industries Anciennes et Régression Régionale* (Colloque de Liège, 22-23 Mai 1964. Librairie Médicis, 1965).

is merely a set of increases in quantities produced. Development is growth plus a favourable change in production techniques and consumer behaviour. Progress is development plus a diminution of social tensions between groups within a society. One of these social tensions is between urban and rural populations. It cannot be solved by the quasi-disappearance of the second. Man has still to feed himself, and half of humanity is undernourished; we have to build the industrial and rural towns of a new world. In any event, we must remember that 'before using ruler and compass it is wise to pose the questions of finality and means' (Pierre Massé). This is in fact the philosophy of prospective.

It is tempting, in this light, to sum up the philosophy of this short book in a single and synthetic word: INTEGRATION. The European Common Market as well as the underdeveloped countries give us the most popular example of this notion, but French or British economies constitute an illustration equally satisfactory.

Spatial integration is indeed one of the major factors which enable us to realize an objective universally desired by both East and West: the reduction of tension amongst human groups. Actually we are already witnessing the birth of large economic organizations composed of more or less integrated subsets.

Growth and development result from a process which increases the degree of interdependence, (1) between industries and social groups, (2) between economic and political regions. In this light it is possible to say that the interdependence of economic sectors is a vertical integration and that regional intercourse is an horizontal integration. Anyhow, the concept of integration is always linked with that of interrelation.

Interdependence can itself be analyzed through existing connections between social groups or economic sectors. It materializes, first, in terms of an observed industrial hierarchy translated through the triangularity of input output matrices. Hierarchy appears, secondly, from the horizontal or regional point of view, through urban polarizations.

This is not the whole story. *Integration*, like Space, has three different aspects:

(a) First, a material aspect which could be called a pure description and which corresponds to the notion of homogeneity similarity of occupation, income level, climate and way of living. A perfectly homogeneous country would appear to be perfectly integrated. But it is the heterogeneity of a region which is the basis of its complementarities. The same heterogeneity is the source, both of social tensions and economic trade. An agricultural region and an industrial region are complementary, but socially opposed. Their economic integration is linked with a sociological and political disintegration which requires explanation. The American Civil War, the problems of dualist economies, and even the present European agricultural question are good examples leading to a second aspect of integration.

(b) The second aspect of integration is formal and is directly linked with interrelation, called connectivity when it is described through connections between the poles of a graph. The degree of connectivity can be measured but constitutes only one element of formal integration. Functional hierarchy through polarization or triangulation is indeed more important.

The third and last element of formal integration is that of vulnerability. A society threatened by a schism is not deeply integrated. A graph would reveal a bottle-neck through which the economy could be split into two parts. But it must not be forgotten that integration is not an end in itself and is valuable only in terms of its objectives. This is why we have to discover a third aspect of integration.

(c) The third aspect of integration is the result of human will and is linked with the objectives striven for by the different regions of an economic organization, be it a National State or a Supra-national Community. It is the compatibility of regional plans (from the point of view of production) coupled with the convergency of regional aims (from the point of view of choice) that is the measure of integration. Integration appears as agreement of an increasing majority on common means and ends. The concept of integration is linked with social and economic progress. From the point of view of territorial collectivities, integration is often conceived as a process creating a social consensus, and through which a community is subsequently formed. It is thus possible to speak of integration, as a dynamic concept, when the elements of consensus and political community do not yet exist fully. This is the case of many underdeveloped countries. It is also the case of Europe. It must be stressed that economic integration calls for political integration. There exists an interrelation between them. But this complementarity is in no way natural and automatic. It depends upon the new intrepretation of traditional symbols, and upon the 'discussion about the best methods of advancing common ideals' (Paul Streeten).[15]

[15] Paul Streeten: *Economic Integration European Aspects* (A. W. Sythoff, Leiden, 1961).
See also J. R. Boudeville: *Note sur la Notion d'Integration* (Cahiers de l'ISEA, Serie L No. 14, 1964).

INDEX

accounting
  methods of, 28
  regionalization of national,
    88-96
  social, 53-5, 88
advertising and publicity, 62,
  150-1
AELE, 148
Africa, immigration potential of,
  127
agglomeration planning, 73
aggregation
  micro-, and macro-economics
    and, 6
  of national matrix, 90-2
  problems of, 10n
agriculture, agricultural
  autarchic, 9
  and industrialization, 8, 9, 99,
    121-3
  complex: in Brazil, 98, 99, 119;
    in developed countries, 21;
    industrialization and, 8, 9, 99,
    121-3; in Fourth Plan, 147;
    in France, 97, 99, 100; inte-
    gration of subsidiary industries
    168; in underdeveloped
    countries, 98, 99; in U.S.A.,
    97, 99; modernization of, 99-
    100; regional improvement in,
    21; rest of economy and, 96,
    98-100, 119; social improve-
    ment in, 21; solutions for,
    21, 167-8; structure of, 167;
    triangulation technique for,
    96, 98, 99
  depressed areas, 87
  development poles, 49-50, 168
  incomes, 149
  in industrial countries, 98-9
  labour force, 72-3
  low productivity of, in South-
    west France, 9
  migration, 72-3, 87-8
  percentage employed in, 9
  problem of, 21

agriculture, agricultural—*contd.*
  techniques: economic space
    and, 2; programming and, 21
  towns, 32, 167-8
  villages, 167
aid
  federal, 69
  from rich to poor regions, 104
  operational zones for financial,
    159-61
ALALC, 14, 44, 111
Alpes region, 39
Aménagement
  Comités, 52, 155
  Commission National, 76n,
    80-1, 158, 162
  Délegation, 72n, 158-9, 162
  Délégué, 162
  Fonds national, 55
  public interest in, 126
  regions of, 18
  significance of, 154-5
America, South (Latin)
  absence of polarization, 86
  Common Market (ALALC), 14,
    44, 111
  immigration potential, 127
  industrialization, 38
  interregional connections,
    119-21
  random aggressiveness, 128
  urbanization, 11, 13, 14
    see also Brazil, Uruguay,
    Venezuela
analysis
  classical dispersion, 24-5
  contiguity, 25-6
  correlation, 26-7
  graph, 9, 10, 28, 29, 30, 38-41
  gravitational, 41-4
  homogeneity, 24-7, 34
  income, 84
  input-output, 54-5, 67
  network, 9
  polarization, 27-32
  structural, 9

approximation, 19, 20, 24, 27, 35, 38, 44, 66, 67, 94

arbitration
and regional wants, 102, 130
between regions, 123-4
functioning of, 134-5
need for, 123
sources of, 56

autonomy, regional
development of, 102-3
Federal experience, 67-9
fiscal and political powers, 55
minimum economic scale, 51
national welfare and, 56
programmes, 51-2
social accounting, 54
welfare and, 102

Auvergne, 27-8, 70

basic employment multiplier, 82-5, 87-8

Bauchet, Pierre, 151n

Belgium
economic cooperation with France, 58
imports-exports and GNP, 147
trade with EEC, 28-30
two programming regions, 51
social accounting, 54

Berge, C., 132n

Berger, Gaston, 15, 136

Bermejo, J. A., 118n

biological homogeneous regions, 3

birth-rate, calculation of, 24

Board of Trade, 47

Bordeaux
as a regional metropolis, 164
as an industrialized pole, 9
50n, 72, 159
employment dominance and dependency, 60

Bouches du Rhône, 3, 5

Boudeville, J. A., 73, 77n, 93n, 96n, 116, 118n, 128n, 171n

Boulding, K., 128n

boundary, boundaries
conflict of, 128-9
definition of a, 37-8

boundary, boundaries—contd.
determination of regional, 23, 32-3, 45, 86-7
graph analysis and determination of, 38-41
influence of contiguity and, 27
in U.S.A., 32-3
movement: and sphere of influence, 58; between homogeneous regions, 33; classical example of, 36-7; dynamic aspects of, 33, 44-5; forecast of, 40-1; gravitational analysis and, 41-4; in Brazil, 11, 13, 14; migration of industry and, 37; population growth and, 44; sociological and economic structure of towns, 44; spatial, 37; tariff reduction and, 44; transport routes and 44
of polarized regions, 38
polarization, 41-2, 58, 108
policy, medium and long-term, 162-3
scheme, 108
villages, 42-3

Brasilia, 124n

Brazil
absence of land reform in, 37
agricultural complex, 98, 99, 119
availability of statistics, 67
boundary movement in, 11, 13, 14
Common Market (ALALC), 44, 111
overall and regional growth, 20-1
polarization models, 11, 13, 14, 118-23
Sudene Plan, 20
urbanization in Rio Grande do Sul, 11-14, 99, 111, 118

Brest, 50n, 159

Brittany, 55, 164

Bye, Maurice, 127n, 168

Cahen, Lucienne, and Claude Ponsard
direct enquiry, 94-5

Cahen, Lucienne, and Claude
  Ponsard—*contd.*
  *La Repartition Fonctionnelle de la
    Population*, 83n, 85n
Cahiers de l'ISEA, 28n, 42n, 93n,
  94n, 171n
Canada
  availability of statistics, 67
  economic cooperation with
    U.S.A., 61
  economic diversity in, 67
  economic influence of U.S.A.
    on, 68
  federal aid in, 69
  political/economic borders, 58
  regional autonomy in, 55
  regional income growth, 68
  social accounting, 55
capital
  coefficients, 54, 86, 103, 122,
    143-4, 145-6
  flow, 73
  migration of, 37, 57
  social overhead, 129
  substitution of, for labour, 103
Cassel, 82n
Caudillo, 128
CECA, 144
Central France, 9
CEREN, 90, 96
CES, 140, 149, 150, 151-2, 158
CFDT (CFTC), 137
chemical commission, 138
Chenery, H. B., 104, 105-7
Cherbourg, 50n, 159
Chevry, Gabriel, 24n
choice
  of instruments, 18
  of objectives: importance of, 51;
    in Fourth French Plan, 150,
    151-2
cities
  hierarchy of, 9, 10-11
  structure of, 10
  see also hierarchy, towns
classical dispersion analysis, 24-5
Clermont Ferrand, 12, 14
cluster method, 33, 34-6
CNAT
  method, 71, 80-2

CNAT—*contd.*
  objectives of, 81
  regionalization of foreign trade,
    95
  urban structure group, 81
coalmining, 49, 62
Cole, W., 31
Columbia River Scheme, 61
commercial gravitation, *see* Reilly's
    Law
commerce and urbanization, 10
Commission de Dévelopement
    Economique, 52
Commission Nationale d'Amén-
    agement, 77, 80-1, 95, 158,
    162
common markets
  abolition of customs, 111
  competition with, 57
  development of national space,
    1
  France's position in, 100
  EEC, 28-9, 34, 49, 57, 67, 100,
    147-8, 169
  reduction of tariffs, 44
  South American (ALALC), 14,
    44, 111
competition
  among regional enterprises,
    102
  between regions, 56, 57, 58, 65
  extension of influence, 58
  factors leading to, 104
  imperfect, 55-6, 57, 123
  oligopolistic, 102
  peaceful, 127
  types of, 126-7
  welfare as objective of, 57
complementarity of regions, 65,
    170 ·
concentration
  index, 114n
  measurement of, 114
  oligopolistic, 117-18
  ratio, 92-4
concepts and definitions, 1-21
concertation
  decisions, 16, 64
  technique, 82
concerted economy, 136

Condorcet problem, 131-4
conflict
    between decision centres, 130-1
    ecological, 128
    of borders, 128-9
    of policies, 1
    tariff, 129
    terms of trade, 126
conflicting instruments, 56-7
Conseil d'Etat, 140, 150n
consumption
    coefficients, 103
    collective, 142
contiguity
    absence of, in economic space,
        3, 16, 28
    analysis, 25-6
    constraint of, 8, 36, 86, 87
    correlation analysis, 26-7
    homogeneity and, 7, 8, 25
    measuring influence of, 25-7
    of economic regions, 3, 7, 8, 16,
        24, 28
cooperation
    basis of, 61
    dominance through, 60-1, 127
    economic; between Belgium and
        France, 58; between Canada
        and U.S.A., 61
    in industrial change, 62
    interregional: problem of, 58,
        60-2, 64-74, 134; medium-
        term growth and, 65-9
    protection, grabbing and, 60-1,
        127
coordination
    benefits of, 65
    between decision centres, 16,
        130, 131
    between regional and national
        efforts, 63-4
    between regional and national
        plans, 47, 50-1
    decentralization and, 16
    lack of, in incentives scheme,
        143
    of investment decisions, 46-7
    of regional investment, 157
    of regional planning, national,
        56-7

coordination—contd.
    practical difficulties of, 65-6
    regional scale, 64
correlation
    analysis, 26-7
    coefficients, 27, 43, 87
cost of living levels, 21, 22, 27
Cumbernauld, 18
cyclical fluctuations, 15, 66

Deane, Phyllis, 31
decentralization
    administrative, 58, 135, 155
    coordination and, 16
    of regional planning, 51-6, 58
decision(s)
    centres: coordination between,
        16, 130, 131; location of, 16
    economic, as programming
        space, 16
    models, 16, 76, 77, 86, 104, 131
    programmes, 137-41
definitions and concepts, 1-21
Delbes, 42
Delouvrier, P., 73
demography, 28, 30-1
Denmark, economic regionalism
    in, 51, 54
départements
    as a set, 8
    evolution of, 8-9
    income per capita, 3, 5
    map of, 3, 4
    role in programming, 46
    stages of development of, 8-9
depopulation, 70-1
depressed areas, 47, 63, 76, 87
development
    areas: high, 8-9; new, 9
    block, 116
    districts, 47
    growth, progress and, 76, 168-9
    national, objectives of, 48-9
    of national space, 1
    poles: creation of, in under-
        developed countries, 24; in
        agriculture, 49-50, 168;
        industrial, and the new
        frontiers, 37-8; in France, 50;

development—*contd.*
  in Italy, 50, 107; in the
    French Plans, 69, 71-2;
    planning of industrial, 48,
    49-50; policy for spontaneous,
    48-9; regional metropolises
    and, 81-2; structural analysis
    of, 9
  regions, 46-7
  short, medium and long-term,
    46-7
  techniques required for, 76
differential effect, 70, 106
differentiation coefficients, 32
disequilibrium, transmission of,
    65
dispersion
  analysis, classical, 24-5
  minimization of, 7-8
distance elasticity, 31, 42, 43, 44
Distribution of Industry Act, 47
Dittrich, E., 130n
dominance
  dependency and, employment,
    58, 60
  of industrialized groups, 58-60
  of poles, 29, 30
  of towns, 32
  through grabbing, protection
    and cooperation, 60-1, 127
Duncan, O. D., 26
Dunn *et al.*, 77
Dunn method, 77-9

economic
  concept of environment, 2
  idea of space, 1, 6
  region and space, 3, 6
  space and regional planning, 1
  structure of regions, 46, 52
  studies: on EEC, 67; tools for
    regional, 22-45
  tools for programming, choice
    of, 18-19
EEC
  and French trade, 100, 147-8
  as example of integration, 169
  as large regional market, 57
  as polarized set, 34

  M

EEC—*contd.*
  coalmining in, 49
  economic studies on, 67
  external trade in, 28
  global polarization of, 29
  total trade flows of, 28-9
Egypt, 98
emigration
  factor, 104
  rural, 87
employment
  analysis, 84-5
  and CNAT aims, 81
  and proportional effect, 70-1
  as aim of welfare, 57, 63
  as basic tool, 77
  based on income analysis, 84
  classification of, 83-4
  dominance and dependency, 58,
    60
  extra-regional control of, 58-60
  factors in regional, 70-1
  French figures, 71
  growth of, in France, 81
  in European countries, 144,
    147
  in propulsive and other indus-
    tries, 66-7
  local, and the location of
    industry, 47
  maintenance of full, 63, 76
  models, 77-85
  multiplier, basic, 82-5, 87-8
  multiplier on global level, 84-5
  percentage growth of, 48
  projected and prospective, 81-2
  rate of growth and, 145-6
England, *see* U.K.
environment, 1, 2
equality, as an object of program-
    ming, 18
equilibrium
  and growth models, 103
  general, 6
  metropolis, 72
  partial, 6
export parameters, 10
Europe
  as economic unit, 64
  trade, 29

FDES, 143, 157
federal states
  financial autonomy in, 55
  interstate trade flows, 67
  powers of central government, 63
  programming in, 16, 56
  regional problems in, 67-9
  social accounting in, 55
FIAT, 157n
financial flows, 23
flows
  comparison of, 29
  intensity of, 103
  interregional trade, see interregional
  network of, 10
  representation of economic, 28-9
fluctuations
  cyclical, 15, 66
  elimination of, 103
  smoothing of, 15
  transmission of, 66-7
Fonds National d'Aménagement du Territoire, 55
forecast
  and prospective philosophy, 14-15, 80
  defined, 15
  different types of, 88
  investment, 64
forward linkage, 115-17
Fox, K. A., 96n
Fourastié, J., 144n
France
  agricultural complex, 97, 99, 100
  aid zones, 159-61
  autonomous regional programming, 51
  concept of forecasting and prospective philosophy, 15
  cooperation with Belgium, 58
  definition of concentration ratios, 92-4
  departements of, 3, 5
  economic regions of, 51
  employment dominance, 59-60
  European cooperation, 64
  external trade with EEC, 28-30
  foreign trade, 28-30, 147-9

France—contd.
  homogeneous regions, 5, 8-9, 35
  homogeneous vertebrate regions, 3
  income per capita, 3, 5
  industrial: census, 53, 91; population, 27-8
  interindustrial matrix, 98
  minimum salary scale, 21
  mobility of labour in, 9, 72-3
  national growth rate, 78
  polarization: map, 17; regions, 12, 14, 24-5
  position in EEC, 100
  railway transport, 66, 90
  rate of growth compared with other countries, 144-7
  regional studies, 103
  social accounting, studies in, 54
  suitability of Marczewsky analysis, 79-80
  telephone communication, 38-40
  triangulation of national matrix, 98
  verification of Reilly's law, 42-4
  West, see West France
  West-East interregional matrix, 100-1
French planning
  backwardness of West, 70-1
  decision centres, 16
  democracy in, 149-53
  development: poles, 50; regions, 47
  employment in, 81, 83
  Fifth French Economic Plan: administration of, 161-2; incomes policy, 148-9; international trade, 147; financial aid, 159-61; long-term aspect, 154, 161-71; medium-term regionalization, 154, 155-61; National Economic Development Council and, 137; Parliamentary approval for, 150; programme in monetary values, 148-9; prospective philosophy in, 161; regionalization of investment, 158-61; regional planning, 154; zones

French planning—*contd.*
of financial aid, 160
financial institutions, 156-7
Fourth French Economic Plan:
administrative procedure,
140-1; agricultural complex,
97, 99, 100; as guide to national objectives, 141, 143-7;
bureaucratic structure, 152-3
choice of objectives,150,151-2;
Commissariat au Plan, 137,
142, 152; discussion of, 136-
53; effectiveness of, 141-9;
enforcement of, 150-1; financial incentives, 142-4; international trade, 147-8; investment in public sector, 141-2;
Modernization Commissions,
137, 138-9, 140, 150; objectives of, 140-1; Parliament,
role of, 140, 149-53; period
of, 136; powers of bureaucracy, 150; process of, 151-2;
programmes and the decision,
137-41; prospective and concerted economy, 136; rates
of growth compared, 145-7;
regional coordination of
investment, 157-60; role of
CES, 149, 150, 151-2; series of
French planners, 144; special
incentives, 142-3; statement
of intentions, 140-1; subsidies, 142-3, 159; tools of,
141; use of the region in, 48
importance of towns, 73-4
incentives, 49, 50, 141-3, 157,
158-9
long-term, 69-73, 81, 154, 161-
171
machinery for, 16
national: character of, 76-7;
involvement in, 154-5; level
of, 47
Paris as polarized region, 71
possible metropolises, 72, 164-7
préfet regional, 19, 52, 152,
155-6, 157, 158
programming regions, 16, 17,
18, 46-7

French planning—*contd.*
public opinion and, 15
regional, 154-71
regional organization, 155-6
Second Plan, 154, 155
sectoral localized analysis, 16
time-lag in regional, 64
frontier
American, disappearance of,
32-3
boundary movement, 36-7
definition of, 37-8
immigration into a, 37-8, 62-3
New, as an economic space,
32-3, 36
Scottish Border as, 37
functional flow diagrams, 60
Furtado, Celso, 20n

Galbraith, 149
Geary, R. C., 25, 26
geography
and the frame of French prospective, 70-2
environment in, 2
idea of space, 1, 2, 6
homogeneity in, 7
notion of polarization, 9
notion of urban hierarchy, 31
techniques for maximizing
objectives, 23
geopolitics, 1
Germany
creation of development poles,
50
external trade with EEC, 28-30
foreign workers in, 64
geographers, 31
growth of economy, 144-6
imports/exports and GNP, 147
increase in employment, 146
'Leitbild' theory, 130
planning bureau, 152
regional autonomy in, 55
social accounting in, 55
Giraud, L., 42n
Glenrothes, 18
GNP, 124-5, 144-7, 148
Gottmann, 73

grabbing, protection and coopera-
    tion, 61-2, 127
Grandpierre, A., 167n
Grangemouth and Falkirk, 18
graph analysis
    economic flows and, 28, 29
    in polarization studies, 9, 28, 30,
        38-41
    in study of hierarchy, 10, 28
    in the determination of bound-
        aries, 38-41
Gravier, J. F., 154n
gravitation, law of commercial,
    30-1
gravitational analysis, 41-4
Greece, 34
growth
    agricultural, 99
    and the regional operational
        model, 76
    as spatially heterogeneous, 77
    autonomous regional, and
        welfare, 102
    balanced, 103
    development, progress and, 76,
        168-9
    differential effects of, 78-9
    economic, American and French
        methods, 102-3
    employment, 81
    general problem of, 82
    harmonized, 82, 103-4
    in Brazil, 20-1
    income and, 19-20
    increase in annual, 143-7
    interregional transmission of,
        66-7
    investment and, 19
    long-term regional, 69-74
    medium-term, and inter-regional
        cooperation, 65-9
    models: Chenery, 105-7; har-
        monized, 103-4; hetero-
        geneous, 103-7; polarized,
        103, 107-15; regional, 76;
        uniform, 103
    national, 19
    national and regional, 20, 21,
        77-8, 102-3
    nature of, 77

growth—contd.
    per capita, 20n, 21
    per capita income, 21, 57, 75-6,
        108, 130
    polarization, in industrialized
        countries, 86-7
    poles: and propulsive industry,
        111-15; localization of, in
        Scotland, 18; regional, 11, 71
    proportional effect, 78-9
    rate(s): in European countries,
        144; of rural areas, 21;
        regional and national, 77-8;
        studies of, 67
    regional and national, 20, 21,
        77-8, 102-3
    sectors, choice of, 18
    transfer problem, 104-5
    uniform, 82n, 103, 107
    variables underlying, 52-3
    weighted, 20-1
Grüson, Claude, 137
Guichard, Olivier, 158

Haavelmo, T., 60, 127
Halff, Maurice, 139, 140n, 147,
    150n
Hansen, Alvin, 36
Hansen, Lee, 83n
Hautreux, Jean, 44n, 108, 164
heterogeneity, 170
heterogeneous
    growth models, 103-7
    regions, 14
hierarchical decision diagrams, 60
hierarchy
    formal description of, 28-30
    regional: absence of, 29; and
        national objectives, 19-21;
        techniques for determining,
        28-30
    urban: concept of, 9, 10-11;
        dominance of metropolis over
        satellites, 32; factors deter-
        mining, 31; importance of,
        10; in French planning, 164-6
        168; polarization and, 10, 74,
        168; predetermination of, 28
Higgins, B., 37

Hill, T. P., 144n, 145
Hirsch, Etienne, 144
Hirschman, A. O., 112, 113, 114,
    115
homogeneity
    analysis, 24-7, 34
    and contiguity, 7, 8, 25
    concept of, 7, 8
    income, trade flows and, 34
    minimization of dispersion, 8
    space defined in terms of, 2, 8
homogeneous
    countries, 170
    regions: and the agricultural
        complex, 167; boundary
        movement and, 33; contrasted
        with spaces, 14; constraints
        on, 8; contiguity of, 3, 7, 8,
        25; data defining, 23; defined,
        8-9; determining boundaries
        of, 23, 33-4; difference be-
        tween polarized and, 27-8;
        differentiation between polar-
        ized and, 22-3; discovery of,
        23-4; geographical, 7; micro-
        and macro-economics and,
        7, 8; model, 163-4; number
        of, 8; of France, 5, 8-9, 35;
        plotting, 35-6; polarization
        and, 14, 27-8; state of
        developed countries and, 24
    spaces: economic, 3; derivation
        by cluster method, 35-6; map
        of, 27-8; notion of, 2; number
        of, 8; polarized and, 14
hospitality, 63

immigration
    into a frontier, 37-8, 62-3
    per capita, 37
    potential, 127
imperfect competition, 55-6, 57,
    123
Imperial Chemical Industries, 6,
    47
import(s)
    and exports, 65, 93-5, 147-8
    matrix of, 10
    parameter, 10

incentives
    form of, 49, 50, 142-3
    lack of coordination in scheme,
        143
    special, 141, 142-3
    to regions, 157, 158-9
incitation policy, 49-50
income
    analysis, 84
    classification in basic employ-
        ment multiplier, 84-5
    correlation between levels of,
        27
    difficulty in assessing, 77
    elasticity, 56, 105
    effect of propulsive industries,
        66-7
    equalization of, 18, 67, 68, 69
    growth and, 19-20, 21
    index of national, growth, 68
    in homogeneity analysis, 34
    investment, 85-6
    national and prospective
        philosophy, 15
    per capita: and dispersion
        analysis, 24; growth of, as
        aim of welfare, 57, 75-6, 108,
        130; immigration and, 37-8;
        in Canada, 68; in France, 3-5;
        in Scotland, 51; in U.K., 31-2;
        in U.S.A., 62-3; level of
        agricultural, 85; of poorest
        regions, 56; regional, 25, 33,
        88; studies of regional, 26-7,
        67; transfer problem and
        regional, 104
    policy: in Fifth French Plan,
        148-9; in Fourth French
        Plan, 148, 149;
    rates of growth, 104, 105
    regional and national, 19, 20,
        37, 62
    zones of high, 7
index
    concentration, 114n
    fixed, 33-4
    variable, 33-4
India, agricultural complex in, 98,
    99
indifference surfaces, 2

industrial
    census, 53, 91
    centres, diversification of, 49-50
    change, cooperation required
        for, 62
    complexes, 116
    establishment contracts, 141
    groups, dominance of, 58-60
    growth in underdeveloped
        countries, 99
    inter-industrial matrix, 98,
        99
    location and urbanization, 81
    poles, 9, 18, 50n, 72, 159
    population of France, 27-8
industrialization
    and agriculture, 8, 9, 99,
        121-3
    high, 8
    in South America, 111-12
    in South Italy, 100
    low, 9
    polarization and, 38
    rate of, 33
    urbanization and, 10, 31, 107,
        161, 164
industry, industries
    aid to, 159
    commission, 138
    diversification of, 31-2
    economic space and, 2
    in developing countries, 21
    interrelated, 116
    Italian investment in, 105, 107
    key regional, 113
    local taxation and, 129
    new and polarized, 114
    oligopolistic concentration of,
        112
    polarization: and satellite, 115;
        in U.S.A., 32-3
    propulsive: analysis, 65;
        characteristics of, 112; de-
        fined, 66, 112; effects of,
        66-7; establishment of, 37;
        growth poles and, 111-12; in
        propulsive regions, 41; local-
        ization of, 18; long-term
        growth and, 73; mutation of
        structure and, 121-3; polari-

industry, industries—contd.
        zation effect and, 113-14;
        polarized growth models and,
        107; production of, 114
    satellite and forward linkage,
        115-16
    structure of, 27
influence
    spheres of, 58
    zones of, 1
    see also polarization
input-output
    analysis, 54-5, 67, 90-1
    coefficients, 84, 90-1
    employment multipliers and,
        83-5
    flows and polarized space, 2-3,
        10
    import substitution and, 114
    interregional, matrix for energy,
        90
    matrix, 40, 90, 107
    national and regional, 91-2
    satellite industries and, 115
    table, 10
    triangulation of, 96, 98, 99
INSEE, 66, 137
instruments
    choice of, 18
    conflicting, 56-7
    of policy and prospective
        models, 16
    supporting, 56, 57-8, 64
integration, 169-71
intensity map, 11
interregional
    arbitration, 123-4
    competition, 56, 57, 58, 65
    connections in South America,
        119-21
    cooperation, 58, 61-2, 64-74,
        134
    economic relations, 126-7
    interdependence, 8, 10, 67
    inverted matrix, 120
    matrix, West-East, 100-1
    model, 104
    trade flows: and national, 89-95;
        breakdown of imports, 95-6;
        concentration ratios, 92-3;

interregional—*contd.*
  cluster analysis, 35; description of, 65-6; determination of, 45; foreign trade, 95; imports and exports, 65, 93-6; instability of, 65; models, 65; multiplier, 67; production and consumption, 95; transportation and, 65-6, 93-4; variation of, 66
  transmission of fluctuations, 66-7
inverted income matrix, 120
investment
  breakdown of, by localized plants, 53
  collective, 141-2, 149
  coordination of regional, 46-7
  decisions, coordination of, 46-7
  economic, 149
  encouraging further investment, 56, 116
  figures, 53
  flows, liberalization of, 73
  forecasting, 64
  guided by objective function, 115
  income and, 85-6
  in Fourth French Plan, 141-3
  initiatory, 116
  in public services, 141-2
  national, in regional planning, 48
  polarization, 56
  private: encouragement of, 49, 50; estimates of, 52-3
  programming and, 19, 87
  public: allocation between regions, 48-9, 85, 88; basic, 48-9, 104; commission dealing with, 138; estimates of, 52; regional planning and, 19, 52, 157-61; requirements and growth models, 107; polarization effect of, 142; to attract development, 48, 50; types of, 157-8; transfer of basic, 104
  rate of growth in, 145-7
  regionalization of, in national

investment—*contd.*
  planning, 85-8, 158-61
  residential, 116
  share in GNP, 145-6
  social, 149
  trusts, regional, 156
  use of subsidies, 50, 67, 69, 100-1, 142-3, 159
Ires *et al.*, 117n
Isard, W., 77n
Isard-Reilly law, 108-9
Italconsult, 117n
Italy
  development poles in, 50, 107
  increase in employment, 146
  industrialization in Southern, 100, 105
  long-term development regions, 47
  polarization and homogeneity, 34
  propulsive industries and employment, 66
  rate of economic growth, 144, 145
  subsidies to poorer regions, 69, 104
  trade with EEC, 28, 29
  see also *Mezzogiorno*

Kennedy administration, 32-3, 36
Keynes, 64, 82, 83, 84

labour
  force: and homogeneous regions 23; breakdown of industry by, 22; decline of British, 31; European, 64; planned movement of, 48; studies of, 52
  influence exerted through control of, 58-60
  migration of, 37, 49, 57, 62-3
  mobility of: costs of, 49; economic change and, 62-3; in France, 9, 72-3; stimulating development, 48
  substitution of capital for, 103
  tertiary, 31-2

Lainé, M. Bloch, 143
Lamour, Philippe, 154n
Lampard *et al.*, 77n
land reform, 37
La Rochelle, 50n, 159
Latin America, *see* America, South
Le Creusot, 8, 9
Le Filâtre, 27, 59, 60, 71
Leitbild, 130
Leontief, W.
    attraction model, 92
    basic employment multiplier,
        67, 82n, 83, 84
    coefficient, 36
    Isard-Leontief technical matrix,
        40
    multiplier effect, 112
    Reilly's law and, 45, 108, 109,
        110
Lille
    employment dominance and
        dependency, 60
    income *per capita*, 3, 5
    regional metropolis, 164
Limbourg, 115
Limoges, 50n, 159
linear programming, 19-20, 121,
    124
loans
    from Fonds National, 55
    to industry, 50
    under Fourth French Plan,
        142-3, 159
Local Employment Act (1960), 47
localization of industry, 18, 21
Loi Minjoz, 55
Lombardini, S., 66-7, 117n
London, 125
long-term
    boundary policy, 162-3
    growth, regional, 69-74
    loans, 157
    programming: economic tools
        of, 72-4; geographic frame of
        French, 70-2; policy, 154,
        161-71; regions, 47, 81, 163;
        time required for, 69-70
Lorient, 50n, 159
Lorraine region, 79, 115
Lot, 5

Lyon
    as a newly developing region, 9
    as a polarized region, 11, 12
    as developing zone to Marseilles,
        163
    employment distribution, 94n
    polarization of, 14
    regional metropolis, 164
    research group, 42
    telephone communication, 38-
        40
    trade flows in, 93-4
    wage earners in, 59-60

Mackinder, 1
macro- and micro-economics, 6-7,
    8
Marczewsky, J., 77, 79-80
market(s)
    macro-economics and, 6n
    North African, 9
    subdivision of territorial, 7
Marseilles
    employment dominance and
        dependency, 60
    income *per capita*, 3, 5
    in development plans, 163
Massé, Pierre, 69, 136, 137, 144,
    169
mathematics, mathematical
    idea of space, 1, 2, 30
    operators, 2, 6
Matilla, 116
matrix
    aggregation, 10n, 90-2
    interregional, for energy, 90
    inverted interregional, 120
    Isard-Leontief technical, 40
    of economic structure, 16
    of imports, 10
    of total EEC trade, 29-30
    West-East interregional, 100-1
Mazamet, 8
medium-term
    boundary policy, 162-3
    development, machinery for,
        46-7
    growth and interregional
        cooperation, 65-9

medium-term—*contd.*
  regionalization, 154, 155-61
  regions, 163
metropolis(es)
  creation of new, 50
  importance of planning, 73
  growth of, 72
  increase in influence of, 58
  influence through labour, 58-60
  number and shape of, 81-2
  plan for regional, 10-11, 164-7
  regions of, 73
  transportation network, 73-4
Meyer, John, 2n, 22n, 28n
Mezzogiorno, il, 50, 69, 100, 104-7
migration
  agricultural, 72-3, 87-8
  international, 127
  of capital, 37, 57
  of industry, 37
  of labour, 37, 49, 57, 62-3
  probable increase in, 127
Minas-Espirito Santo, 20
micro- and macro-economics, 6-7,
  8
mineral resources, 8
Molière, 26
Monnet, Jean, 51, 144
Montevideo, 14, 118, 119, 120
Muth *et al.,* 72n
Myrdal, G., 112n

Nantes, 50n, 159, 164
national
  accounting, regionalization of,
    88-96
  and regional growth, 20, 21,
    77-8, 102-3
  and regional hierarchy, 19-21
  coordination of regional plan-
    ning, 56-7
  development, objectives of, 48-9
  Economic Development Coun-
    cil, 47, 137
  efforts, coordination between
    regional and, 63-4
  growth, 19, 77-8
  growth rate, 144-7
  income, 15, 19, 20, 37, 62

national—*contd.*
  income growth, 68
  input-output, 91-2
  investment, 48, 85-6, 158-61
  involvement in planning, 154-5
  matrix, aggregation of, 90-2
  objectives, Fourth French Plan
    as guide to, 141, 143-7
  plans, coordination between
    regional and, 47, 50-1
  productivity, 21, 131, 144, 146
  resources, variation in, 19
  space, development of, 1
  trade flows, 89-95
natural resources
  and long-term growth, 73
  exploitation of, 8, 9, 86
neighbourhood, 11
Netherlands
  development centres in, 50
  national character of planning
    in, 76
  polarized set within EEC, 34
  trade with EEC, 28, 29, 30
  two programming regions for,
    51
new
  frontier, 32-3, 36
  towns, 24, 50, 76, 166
North African market, 9
North America, *see* Canada, U.S.A.
Nurkse, R., 103, 104n

objectives
  choice of: importance of, 51;
    in Fourth French Plan, 150,
    151-2; of regional, 130-1
  clash between regional and
    national, 19
  Fourth French Plan as guide to
    national, 141, 143-7
  of Fourth French Plan, 140-1
  of regional programmes, 46, 57
oligopolistic
  competition, 102
  concentration, 117-18
operational models, regional,
  75-135
Orinoco valley, 24

PADOG, 71, 73, 81n, 159, 161, 163, 164
Paelinck, J., 118n
parameters
    concept of polarization, 10n, 38
P   xport, 10
a⊃renteau, 68, 69
Paris
    as a highly developed zone, 8
    employment dominance and dependency, 60
    growth of region, 71-2, 166
partial equilibrium, 6
Passo Fundo, 11, 13
Pelotas, 11-14, 111-12, 118-21
Perloff *et al.*, 77n
Perroux, François, 2n, 56, 67, 103n, 107, 112, 113, 127n, 136, 147
Piatier, 42
Pinchemel, 166
planning
    allocation of investment in, 85
    decentralization of regional, 47, 51-6
    length of plan and size of programming region, 18
    national, 76-7
    national coordination of regional 56-7
    of French economy, *see* French planning
    regionalization of investment in national, 85-8
polarization
    absence of, in autarchic economies, 24
    absence of, in South America, 86
    analysis, 27-32, 34
    and programming regions, 16, 18
    as a new technique, 65
    as an objective of regions, 57
    assessment of, from telephone calls, 38-40
    boundary movement and, 11, 12
    causes of nodal influence, 32
    concept of, 9

polarization—*contd.*
    defined, 9-10
    description of extent of, 40
    diversification of activities, 31-2
    dominance of metropolis, 32
    effect, 113-15, 117
    employment and, 70-1
    functional hierarchy through, 170
    geographical, 72
    global, of EEC, 29
    growth models, 107
    heterogeneity and, 14
    hierarchy of cities and, 10-11, 24, 74
    in America, 32-3
    increase of influence through, 58
    industrialization and, 38
    input-output flows and, 2-3, 10
    interdependence and, 10
    investment and, 56, 86-7
    macro- and micro-economics and, 7
    map of France, 17
    models, 118-23, 163
    new industries and, 114
    notions involved in, 10
    of growth in industrialized countries, 86-8
    parametric conception of, 10, 10n
    propulsive industries and, 66-7, 113-14
    public investment and, 142
    Reilly's law and, 41
    satellite industries and, 115
    space and, 2-3
    traffic and, 11
polarized
    prospective models, 163
    regions: absence of, in underdeveloped countries, 24; defining, 38; determining boundaries, 23, 33; differentiation between homogeneous and, 22-3; discovering, 23-4; economic relations defining, 23; extension of, 30, 75-6; fitting new towns into, 24; flows between, 110-11; form-

polarized—*contd.*
  ation of, 14; formation of a
    new frontier and, 37-8; graph
    analysis and, 38-41; gravita-
    tional analysis and, 41-4;
    growth models and, 107, 108;
    homogeneous and, 14, 27-8; in
    industrialization and, 38; in
    French regional studies, 103;
    in new countries, 38; in old
    countries, 38; of Brazil, 11,
    13, 14; of France, 11, 12, 24-5
    of Lyon and Clermont, 11,
    12; programming, 38
  space: defined, 2-3, 9-10, 29;
    growth models and, 103,
    107-15; homogeneous and, 14
poles
  development, *see* development
  growth, 11, 18, 71, 111-15
  industrialized, 9, 18, 50n, 72,
    159
  satellite, 30
policy, policies
  conflict of, 1
  incomes, 148-9
  instruments of: choice of, 18-
    19; prospective models and,
    16
  national: coordination of, 56;
    regional, 19-21
  regional: economic, 55-6;
    objective of national, 19-21
  welfare as objective of, 19, 57,
    75-6, 130
Ponsard, C., 83n, 85n
population
  and employment in Lyon area,
    60
  dynamic, 41-2
  growth: and boundary move-
    ment, 44; and unemployment
    rate, 68; rates in France, 72
  intensity flows and, 109
  maintenance of minimum, 87-8
  of France, 164
  of towns, 30-1
  size of, for regional planning,
    51
  static, 4

population—*contd.*
  studies, 52
  trends, study of, 70-1
  urban and rural tensions, 169
Porto Alegre, 11, 13, 14, 118-21
'poster' technique, 50
power, as an objective of program-
    ming, 18
Prate, Alain, 49
Préfet régional, 19, 52, 152, 155-6,
    157, 158
private investment, 49, 50, 52-3
productivity, national, 21, 131,
    144, 146
programmes
  decision, 137-41
  regional economic, 46-74
programming
  agricultural techniques and, 21
  autonomous, 51-2
  establishment of, 87
  in federal states, 16, 56
  in France, 16, 17, 18
  institutions for, 161-2
  linear, 19-20, 121, 124
  long-term, 47, 69-74, 81, 154,
    161-71
  national, 16, 47
  objectives of, 18
  polarized regions and, 38
  progress in, 76, 103, 168-9
  regions: and development
    regions, 46-7; defined, 16;
    factors involved in, 46;
    French, 16, 17, 18, 51-2; size
    of, 46, 51; size of and length
    of plan, 18, 46-7, 75
  space: defined, 2-3, 16; micro-
    and macro-economics and, 7;
    non-contiguity of, 16
progress, growth and develop-
    ment, 76, 168-9
proletarianism, regional, 56, 62-4,
    70
proportional effects, 70-1, 105-
    106
propulsive
  firms, 117
  industry, *see* industry
  structure, 112-13

prospective
  employment, 82
  models, 16, 77, 80, 163
  philosophy: as a policy, 14-15,
    161; concerted economy, 136;
    contrasted with forecasting,
    14-15, 80; definition of, 14;
    effect of, 169; executive body
    for, 161-2; in French Plans,
    136, 161
  planning, 143
  remodelling, 161-9
protection, grabbing, cooperation
  and, 61-2, 63-4, 127
Provence, 9
public investment, see investment
purchasing power, 7, 21

quasi-*contrats* 50, 140-1, 143,
  153

Radner, 82n
railways, 48, 66, 90
Rasmussen, P. N., 113, 114
regional
  accounting, 23, 88-9
  and national hierarchy, 19-21
  autonomy, see autonomy
  boundaries, determining, 32-3
  Commission for Economic
    Development, 156, 158
  constraints, 87-8
  decentralization of planning, 47,
    51-6, 58
  Development Societies (SDR),
    156
  economic programmes, 46-74
  economic studies, tools for,
    22-45
  Expansion Committee, 155, 156
  firms, encouragement of, 47
  growth: and national, 20, 21,
    77-8, 102-3; long-term, 69-
    74: rate, 77-8; social account-
    ing and, 53-4; studies of, 103;
    variables in, 52-3
  incitation policy, 49-50
  income, size of, 22

regional—*contd.*
  inequality, 56-7
  institutions and organizations,
    154-59
  interdependencies, 67
  interests, divergence of national
    and, 56
  investigation, 23
  investment, 156-7
  mechanism for programming, 23
  metropolises, 72, 164-7
  minimum economic size for
    programming, 51
  need for interdependence, 169
  operational: models, 75-135;
    research, 23
  objectives, 75-6, 129-35
  planning, French, 154-71
  proletarianism, 56, 62-4, 70
regionalism
  economic, 48
  measuring influence of, 25-7
  gionalization
  evolution of, 155-6
  functioning of, 157-61
  medium term, 155-61
  models, 75-7
  of foreign trade, 95-6
  of income and activity, 85-101
  of investment, 85-8
  of national accounting, 88-96
  of national input-output matrix,
    88-96
regionalizing
  a national plan, 47-51
  employment models, 77-85
regions
  and subsidies, 100
  and the national plan, 47-8
  as opposed to space, 3
  cooperation in, 60-2
  coordination of, 63
  employment dominance of,
    59-60
  heterogeneous, 14
  homogeneous, see homogeneous
  increase in influence, 58
  polarized, see polarized
  programming, see programming
  protection of, 60-1

regions—*contd.*
  underdeveloped, 118-23
  usefulness of çoncept of, 48, 63-4
regression
  coefficients, 27, 44
  formula, 43, 87
Reilly's law, 14, 30-1, 41-5, 108-9, 112
Rhône
  département, 42-3
  region, Alpes-: and distribution of employment, 94n; and national accounting, 88; growth rate, 78; inter-industry and social accounting, 54, 55; linear transport model, 93; polarization in, 27-8; regionalism, economic, 51; telephone relations in, 40
  valley, 9, 62
Rio Grande do Sul, 11, 13, 14, 20-1, 98, 99, 111-12, 118-23
Rio-Guanabara-São Paulo, 20-1
road
  traffic: intensity of, 11; polarization and, 11, 14, 27, 38
  transport, revolution, 154
roads, as basic public investment, 48, 69
Robine, Michel, 43
Rochefort, M., 164
Roger's index, 114n
Rolls Royce, 47
Rome, Treaty of, 144, 150n
Roubaix, 60, 164
Ruhr, 115

SAFER, 167
Saint-Etienne, 8, 9, 40, 60, 62, 94n, 164
Saint-Nazaire, 8, 9, 164
Samuelson, P., 82n, 103n
Saône valle y, 9
satellite
  industry and forward linkage, 115-17
  poles, 30
  towns, 10, 41, 58, 73, 87

SCET, 157
scientific research, 127-8, 161
Scotland
  awareness and economic development, 58
  economic frontiers and, 37
  Development Group, 19
  linear programming model in, 124-6
  localization of growth poles in, 18
  new towns and polarization, 18, 24
  regional programme for, 48n, 51
  size suitable for economic regionalism, 51, 54
  social accounting in, 55
SEEF, 90, 137, 144
Sema, 117n
Sengupta, J. K., 98
Seine, 5
sets, mathematical, 6-7, 8
SMIG, 21
SNCF, 66
social
  accounting, 53-5
  overhead capital, 129
SODIC, 143
SOFICEMA, 143
Solow, R., 82n, 103n
South-West France, 9
space
  as opposed to region, 8
  concepts of, 1-2
  complementarity of, 14
  dispersion analysis of, 24-5
  economic, 1, 2, 3
  emotive connotation of, 1, 2
  geographic, 1, 2
  homogeneous, 2, 7, 36
  mathematical, 1, 2
  polarized, 2-3, 9-10, 14, 29
  programming, 2-3, 16
  relation of economic to mathematical and geographic, 2, 6
Spain, 34
Stone, Richard, 89n, 106n
Streeten, P., 171
Strout, A., 108n

subsidies
　competition to obtain, 129
　in Canada, 67, 68, 69
　regional trade and, 100-1
　under Fourth French Plan,
　　142-3, 159
Sudene Plan, 20
supporting instruments, 56, 57-8,
　64
Sweden
　national planning in, 76
　growth rate, 144
Switzerland
　economic regionalism, 51
　foreign labour in, 64
syndicalism, 27

tariffs, 44, 129
technical
　coefficients, 89, 103, 117
　schools, 24
teleological concepts, 8, 15
telephone calls as indication of
　polarization, 38-40
terms of trade conflict, 126
tertiary
　employment in Britain, 31-2
　growth and agricultural
　　migration, 87
textile workers in U.S.A., 26-7
Tiebut, Charles, 83n
time-horizon, 46, 69
Tinbergen, J., 57n, 58, 64, 110
tools
　for regional economic studies,
　　22-45
　for regional programming, 46-7
　of the Fourth French Plan, 141
Toothill, J. N., 48n
Toulouse, 50n, 159
tourism, 9, 88, 142
towns
　absence of new, in France, 166
　and neighbourhood concept, 11,
　　30
　Cahen-Ponsard enquiry, 94-5
　differentiation of, 11
　demographic importance of,
　　30-1, 32, 44

towns—contd.
　diversification of functions, 30
　evolution of, 11-14
　function of, 73-4
　graph analysis and, 38-9
　gravitational analysis and, 41-2
　growth rate of, 41-2, 44
　importance of production
　　changes in, 44
　influence of demographic
　　growth of, 11
　intensity of flows between,
　　108-11
　manpower employed in large
　　French, 94
　metropolises, 72, 81, 165
　of Central and South-West
　　France, 9
　polarization and, 30
　satellite, 10, 41, 58, 73, 87
　sectors of employment in, 83
　small, 9
　structure of, 11, 44
　types and influence, 32
　urban hierarchy, see hierarchy
trade flows
　EEC, 28-30
　interregional see interregional
　interstate, 67
　polarized, 29, 107-11 ; structure
　　of, 30
trade unions, 51, 64, 137, 150, 152,
　156
traffic
　as guide to polarization, 11, 14,
　　23, 27
　intensity, 12, 13
　index of absolute increment of,
　　11
Tranches Opératoires, 52, 157
transfer problem, 104-5, 107
transport
　and French plans, 141
　cross haulage, 92
　commission dealing with, 138
　costs, 76
　importance of routes, 44, 74
　in Brazil, 11, 13, 129
　linear model, 93-4
　networks, 2, 11, 14, 73

transport—*contd.*
  planning, 74
  public investment in, 141
  railways, 48, 66, 90
  road, 66
Turin, 66-7
Turkey, 34

underdeveloped
  countries: absence of polariza-
    tion in, 24, 119; agriculture
    in, 98-9; industrial growth in,
    99; programming in, 24;
    stagnation in, 36
  regions of France, 163-4
unemployment
  growth of population and, 68
  low level of as political objective,
    24
  need to cure, 63
  recognition of regions through,
    38, 47
  remedies for structural, 49
  studies of regional, 67
Unilever, 47
United Kingdom
  aid from rich to poor regions,
    104
  and new towns, 50, 76, 166
  change in attitude to planning,
    136
  character of planning in, 76
  growth of economy in, 144-6
  income and tertiary employ-
    ment, 31-2
  imports/exports and GNP, 147
  linear programming model in,
    124-6
  Local Employment Act (1960),
    47
  localization of growth poles, 18,
    37
  location of decision centres, 16
  management-union conflict, 64
  National Economic Develop-
    ment Council, 47, 76, 137
  public opinion and planning,
    51
  significance of frontier in, 37

United Kingdom—*contd.*
  stages of economic regionalism
    in, 47, 51
  suitability for Marczewsky
    analysis, 79-80
  zones of urban influence in, 40
unproductive competition, 61, 127
universities, 18, 31, 52, 54, 138,
    161
urbanization
  commerce and, 10
  European, 58
  industrialization and, 10, 31, 81,
    107, 161, 164
  problem of, 9
  rapid, 10, 11
Uruguay
  economic boundary of, 44, 111
  polarization of Montevideo, 14,
    118, 119
Uruguayana, 11
U.S.A.
  agricultural complex in, 97, 99
  correlation analysis, 26-7
  Council of Economic Advisers,
    152
  economic: cooperation with
    Canada, 68; growth, 145;
    influence on Canada, 68
  federalism and programming, 16
  French trade with, 148
  geographical and economic
    frontier, 36-7, 62
  growth and employment
    studies, 77
  homogeneity between European
    countries and, 34
  homogeneous regions in, 32-3
  'New Frontier' policy, 32-3, 36
  political and economic border,
    58
  regional aid, 104
  regional studies, 103
  social accounting, 55
  state and federal economic
    policies, 64

Valéry, Paul, 1
value judgments, 124-6

Venezuela
  and foreign capital, 131
  programming Orinoco valley, 24
vertebrate populations, 3
villages
  attraction of towns, 42-4
  hierarchy of cities, towns, and,
    9, 10
  satellite, 10
Vogelsberg, 50

wages and salaries
  in France, 21
  prices and, 89
Washington, 124n
weighting, 33-5
welfare
  aims of, 57-8
  as an objective of programming,
    18, 75-6
  as an objective of regions, 57,
    130
  autonomous regional growth
    and, 102

welfare—*contd.*
  maximization of national, 76
  problem of social and political,
    19
  subordination of regional
    planning to national, 56
West France
  agriculture in, 100-1
  backwardness of, 9, 70-2
  financial aid for, 159
  metropolises in, 81-2
  poles in, 50n
  underdevelopment of, 163,
    168

Youngson, A. J., 56, 113, 116

zones
  division of France into five,
    159-61
  of influence, changes in, 1
  operational, for financial aid,
    159-60